How to Be Her Best Lover Ever by John Alexander
(c) Copyright 2005, John Alexander Enterprises, Inc.

How to Be Her Best Lover Ever

By John Alexander

Praise for "How to Be Her Best Lover Ever"

"All Women Should Be So Lucky"

Let me tell you about my man, John Alexander To start, John is a GENIUS with his tongue and I come every time.

I can't wait to get naked – in the bedroom, in the kitchen, in the living room, wherever – because I know I'm about to feel the most intense pleasure of my life.

Just when I think I've had the most powerful orgasm ever, he brings me to a place I hadn't thought my body could go. All women should be so lucky to have such an amazing man."

- Samantha, John's Girlfriend

"Two weeks. That's how long it took my husband to become a sexual animal after he got your material. He's 47 years old, so we weren't totally sure it would be possible for him to make love to me as often as you said. **But now we have sex 3 times a day, and before it was only once a week!"**

- Joan S., Peoria, IL

From: Jay **** (j****@nyc.rr.com)
Subject: Your E-Book
Date: June 7, 2005 8:41:43
To: ****@herbestlover.com

Hey John,

Just finished reading your book and I think it has great material in it, with stuff I didn't know. Good solid info for any guy that wants to be better in bed than the last guy she had. I'd recommend it.

Hope you have lots of success with this,
Jay

From: Amy **** (****@columbia.edu)
Subject: WOW
Date: May 28, 2005 11:05:16
To: ****@herbestlover.com

John,

I want you to use this as testimonial on your site.

The sex with my husband Bill had gotten BAD. I was sexually frustrated, because whenever we had sex, it would last for a nanosecond. Well, you've turned Bill into a sexual powerhouse in just a couple of days.

What's more, I didn't think I would EVER swallow his semen. Honestly, his taste made me want to gag. But since Bill made the dietary changes you recommended, it's gone from tasting like soap to being almost like ice cream!

Needless to say, I am a VERY happy woman!

Amy
New York, NY

From: Laura M****** (********@yahoo.com)
Subject: Your E-Book
Date: May 16, 2005 8:30:10
To: ****@herbestlover.com

I wasn't sure that I should buy your guide for my boyfriend, but I'm writing this to you just after having the most tremendous orgasm of my entire life!!! He has taken your advice and IT WORKS. Our sex life is better than I ever thought possible and I am more satisfied than I've ever been.

How to Be Her Best Lover Ever by John Alexander
(c) Copyright 2005, John Alexander Enterprises, Inc.

Table of Contents

Introduction... 8
"AH! AHHHHH!" = Sexual Music.................... 11
Who Can Improve?... 12
Don't Take Sex So Seriously........................... 15
Have The Proper Mindset When You're Having Sex... 17
Become the Casanova of Kissing................... 21
    Your lips.. 22
    When should you go in for the kiss?........... 22
    How to Move in For the Kiss The First Time..... 25
    The Most Important Thing for You to Know About Kissing.. 26
    The Proper Mindset of the Master Kisser......... 27
    Techniques of a Make-Out Master................... 27
Be Proud of Your Body................................... 31
How to Receive The Best Oral Possible........ 34
How to Get Her to Swallow............................ 39
    What to consume:....................................... 40
    What to avoid:... 41
Slowness is Important..................................... 47
    Here's a big secret that will instantly make you a far better lover.. 47
    Every Woman is Unique............................... 48
    The Key to Going Slow 48
Your Health and Diet....................................... 53
Six Aphrodisiacs That Really Work................. 76
    Oysters... 76
    Chocolate... 77
    Cinnamon... 77
    Cloves... 78
    Honey... 78
    Nutmeg... 78
A Woman's Anatomy....................................... 80

How to Be Her Best Lover Ever by John Alexander
(c) Copyright 2005, John Alexander Enterprises, Inc.

Overcoming Sexual Anxiety........................... 82
How to Give Your Woman a Hand Job.......... 88
Guide to Giving Oral...................................... 91
    Learning to Love The Vagina......................... 95
    Your Eating Style.. 97
    The Suction Technique................................. 105
    How to Move Her Towards a Mind-Blowing Orgasm.. 106
    Advanced Tips For Eating Pussy.................. 110
    Tongue Exercises.. 114
    John Alexander's Final Thoughts About Cunnilingus.. 115
Her G-Spot.. 117
How to Insert Your Penis............................ 120
Sexual Positions 122
    The Missionary Position...............................123
    Doggie Style...124
    Girl on Top... 125
    The Pelvis Slam.. 125
    The Ultimate Front-Row View 126
    In From the Side... 126
How to Give Her the Orgasm To End All Orgasms... 128
How to Reduce Your Refractory Period to be the Best Lover She's Ever Had... or Ever Will Have!... 130
    The Biggest Secret to Master the Art of Sex.. 135
Other Guides By John Alexander................ 136

How to Be Her Best Lover Ever by John Alexander
(c) Copyright 2005, John Alexander Enterprises, Inc.

Disclaimer

Some of the exercises in this book involve orgasm. Having an orgasm elevates your heart rate. If you have a heart condition or any other serious medical condition, please consult your physician before beginning this or any other exercise program.

Copyright Notice

©2005 John Alexander Enterprises, Inc.

All rights reserved.

Any unauthorized use, sharing, reproduction, stealing, or distribution of this book by any means is strictly prohibited. Distribution will be prosecuted to the fullest extent of criminal and civil law. The publisher of this book regularly and actively searches the internet for copyright violations.

By reading this book, you agree that when using its material, you will abide by all federal, state, and local laws. You also agree that the author of this material will not be held responsible for any consequences of any irresponsible actions you take.

To put this in plain English, you are responsible for your own behavior, and I expect you to act responsibly!

Now, let's get on with the good stuff.

How to Be Her Best Lover Ever by John Alexander
(c) Copyright 2005, John Alexander Enterprises, Inc.

Introduction

This book is for any man who invests time and effort into becoming the greatest lover a woman could ever have.

There is a common line that says a guy is "getting lucky" when he has sex. He should be happy whenever he gets it, because let's face it, women unfortunately don't need or like sex as much as we do.

This old adage is simply not true. It is a trick guys who are bad in bed use to deflect any bad feeling about their own sexual prowess. After all, one of the worst self-esteem killers is for a man to think he's a bad lover.

However, it's time to drop the ego, admit that maybe you are a bad lover, but acknowledge that there is hope. You can improve.

Time and effort have been wasted in bed with women because of cluttered ideas about what women want, mixed messages from all the sources of "advice" out there, improper ability to read a woman's signals, and just plain poor strategy.

Or maybe you haven't even had ample time in bed with a woman yet. That's okay. By learning from this guide, you will ensure that when the time comes, **you will rock her world!**

There are many gaping holes in the average man's arsenal. Ability to last a sufficient amount of time is one. The cost of poor oral sex skills is also a huge opportunity waster.

There's a large percentage of men who don't even perform oral sex. And many men who do don't enjoy it, which means that cunnilingus is one of the least effective parts of their sexual concoction.

The ineptitude of sexual skills is often masked by the fact that much of the time, sex is initiated by the woman. The woman feels horny, has an available man, and makes herself receptive to sex without, or despite, efforts on his part.

When the sex takes place, she feels really good, but is often disappointed. Hence the common complaints from frustrated women that "sex is overrated."

This reality is why, when they have sex with a horny woman who feels really good, certain men will consider themselves sexual studs, yet when they fail to satisfy, it is always because the woman is frigid, "we'll just never be able to understand women"... or whatever other excuse they use that day.

How to Be Her Best Lover Ever by John Alexander
(c) Copyright 2005, John Alexander Enterprises, Inc.

It is easy to have sexual intercourse. We are biologically preprogrammed to insert our penises into warm, inviting vaginas. The amount of knowledge required to perform the basic sex act is low.

But to become the kind of guy who makes women see fireworks and worship the ground he walks on... and as a consequence, to obtain all the sexual pleasure he could ever want and need... requires effort and learning.

Sexual superstars make women go, "Ah. Ah! AH! AHHHHH!" Because they give women maximum pleasure, they in turn get all the pleasure they could ever possibly desire. If you love sex and want to be a sexual superstar, then this guide is for you.

"AH! AHHHHH!" = Sexual Music

AH! AHHHHH! The universal sound of a woman moaning with sexual pleasure. Other variations are Mmmmmmm and Yessss! It is a deep, animalistic moan from deep within her. Ahhhh when you stimulate her G Spot. Ahhhh when you eat her pussy. Ahhhh when she has an orgasm with your penis inside her.

Ahhhh is the sign of sexual pleasure that's been generated. It's the sound you hear loudly when you lick her tensed clitoris. It's the sound you hear softly when you run your fingers ever so gently and teasingly all over the soft, sensitive skin of her body.

It's your job, first and foremost, to generate that sound in your woman. Most guys know they have to be sexually innovative and sensual, but they just don't do anything new. The moans in their women wither down to mere heavy breathing, and then sighing to want to get it over with.

Just as the smart businessman knows that the things he do are effective only if they ring the cash register, the things you do sexually are effective only if you get that primal reaction.

Who Can Improve?

Anyone can! Get that through your skull. Obviously you realize that self-improvement is possible and will happen as long as you work at it... that's why you bought this book.

It doesn't matter how old you are or how inexperienced you are with sex. It doesn't matter what your penis size is or how tall or short you are. All it takes is for you to be a physically intact man (i.e., you've never been castrated) who wants to have mind-blowing sex, both for yourself and for your partner.

As I explained in the sales letter for this site, you can literally become the best lover a woman has ever had, in only minutes a day.

There are basically two ways you will accomplish this:

1. By learning the proper techniques. Go slow, be attuned to the woman's reactions, be passionate, and take the lead in the sexual encounter. I'll give you the step-by-step instructions on how to do everything from eating her out to rocking her world with your rock-hard dick.

2. By transforming yourself into a primal, virile, lustful man. There are a large number of things you can do right now to dramatically boost your body's production of sex hormones and semen, leading to much more powerful erections and the ability for you to orgasm several times a day.

I have sex with my girlfriend at least two times everyday, and sometimes as many as six times. I'm not saying this to brag, but instead to tell you what is possible. I'm incredulous when I see surveys saying that say that the average sexually active person only has sex 2 or 3 times per week.

The bottom line is that by following this guide, you'll be able to have sex 2 or 3 times *a day* or more. Your woman will be entranced by you; it will be as if you are her drug. She'll need another "fix" of you constantly.

In fact, good sex is by far the best cement to both hold together a relationship and to make it a happy one.

(By the way, I use the phrase "your woman" throughout this guide because it's easier than constantly saying "wife" or "girlfriend.")

You have within you a potent and colossal sexual potential. It's just waiting to be developed and unleashed.

When you finish this book, you'll have developed an extraordinary sexual power. You'll have a unique ability to satisfy women far beyond any other guy that the typical chick has ever encountered in her life.

So get ready to... Become Her Best Lover Ever.

How to Be Her Best Lover Ever by John Alexander
(c) Copyright 2005, John Alexander Enterprises, Inc.

Don't Take Sex So Seriously.

This isn't your typical Dr. Ruth-style sex book. I'm going to use dirty words like "pussy" and "dick"... rather than sticking with the clinical terms.

You need to develop a dirty mind. Sex is the greatest pleasure you'll ever find, so relax about it. Enjoy it.

After all, is there anything better in this world to come over and over again inside your woman, who's dripping and trembling with so much lust for you that she screams, "Baby I want your cock so much!"?

As you picture that scenario, I'm sure it brings a smile to your face. And that's the thing... sex should make you smile.

Remember, sex is the most fun you can have doing *anything* in life. It's more fun than skydiving. More fun than partying. More fun than abusing your body with drugs or alcohol.

So allow it to be wonderful and fun for you. Stop taking it so seriously.

One of the biggest complaints I've heard from women over the years (and compliments given to me) is that so many guys take sex way to seriously. They have intense expressions on their face as if they were concentrating for a test.

Fuck that. When you're watching pornography, do you try to "perform" when your hand slips down your pants? Of course not. Instead you just concentrate on a) the pleasure from your hand and b) the visuals of the porn.

It should be the same thing when you have sex. Just focus on the pleasure you're having.

This brings up another point...

How to Be Her Best Lover Ever by John Alexander
(c) Copyright 2005, John Alexander Enterprises, Inc.

Have The Proper Mindset When You're Having Sex

Relax and enjoy it. That's all you need to do. When you're having sex, you should only be thinking about:

- How good your woman's skin feels to touch.
- How good it feels to touch your woman with every part of your body.
- How beautiful and sensual your woman is.
- How good she smells and tastes.
- How much you love the sex because it feels soooo good.

That's it. Now, notice what wasn't on the list? I'll tell you:

1) How well you're performing.

One of the best ways to destroy your full enjoyment of sex is to put pressure on yourself about performing. You can overcome this by...

- **Having no expectations.** Don't think. Turn off the analytical portion of your brain. Make no demands on yourself.
- **Just focusing on your body's senses.** Feel her soft, warm skin, soak your tongue on her pleasant wetness down below, and hear the melody of her

moans. As your brain's occupied with all of that, it won't be sabotaging you with thoughts like, "I wonder if I'll last a long time."

To the extent that you do think about your performance, think about it in the best possible terms. Do affirmations like, **"I am becoming a stallion in the bedroom!"** and **"I am the best lover she will ever have!"**

Because let's face it, one of the best ways to be successful in the bedroom is to have a massive amount of confidence. If you have a strong sense of self-esteem, there's nothing you can't accomplish.

2) How much enjoyment she's getting out of the sex.

If you have thoughts like, "I wonder if she'll come" or "I wonder if this feels good to her when I touch her like that," it means you're thinking too much about your performance.

The time to think about such things is when you're outside of the intercourse, either before the sex takes places, or afterwards.

But while you're having sex, you don't ever want to put pressure on yourself. Putting pressure on yourself causes your, ironically, to get a lot *less* enjoyment out of the sex than she otherwise would, because it also puts subtle pressure on your woman.

So while you're having sex, focus only on the wonderful sensations that you're feeling. Leave any sort of analysis for afterward.

3) Non-sexual stuff, like
- **"I wonder if I'll win that big contract for the company next week."**
- **"God I hate the way that guy honked his horn at me this afternoon."**

When you're having sex, stay in the present moment. Don't think about the past or the future.

After all, you only live life in the present. When you're alone in the bedroom with your woman, all that exists in the world is your body and her body. The past and future are just figments of your imagination at that point. So let them go.

Why it's important to stay focused on the present

To get the maximum amount of pleasure possible from sex, you need to be always focused on and enjoying the sensations your body is receiving.

Because you feel so wonderful, the thought doesn't even cross your mind about having an orgasm (or, worse, whether she'll have one).

You just enjoy the sex for what it is, not for what happens at the end of it.

The whole reason why couples become bored with their sex life is because lovemaking becomes an outcome-dependent activity.

When everything was young and fresh in the relationship, the two lovers basked in each other's bodies. But when they've got a long history together, and they both are thinking about jobs and bills to pay, sex quickly becomes just another chore. When the guy orgasms, the chore is complete.

"Life's a journey, not a destination." That famous quotation applies to sex as well.

When you're having sex, just relax and think about the pleasure your body feels. That's it. Because you feel so good, there's no need to rush! Aaaah, so good!

Become the Casanova of Kissing

Kissing is a crucial part of the sexual process. And yes, kissing *is* a form of sex.

When humans kiss, it triggers a flurry of activity in the brain and adrenal glands that cause a surge in nerve stimulation and sexual excitement all over the body.

Your (and her) adrenaline glands produce norepinephrine, causing feelings of euphoria, and adrenaline, causing your heart to feel like it's fluttering with joy and your body to have that queasy, "this person takes my breath away," feeling.

While all this is going on:
- Both of your sex organs are engorging with blood.
- Your penis swells in size.
- Her vagina becomes wetter.
- Sex hormones surge through both of you, increasing both your horniness and your sense of well-being.

Additionally - and this is an important point - a woman's lips are an **erogenous zone**. She has a high concentration of nerve endings there, making her even wetter with desire for you when you stimulate those nerve endings.

So the bottom line is that not only should you focus heavily on kissing, you should linger with your kisses and keep on kissing the woman throughout the lay.

Your lips

Your lips should be masculine and hungry for the woman. At the same time, try to keep them soft... softer than your instincts tell you to, though not as soft as hers.

Keeping my lips just a bit softer than I used to is one of my secrets to a good kiss. Ever since I've made that change, I've been told by women that I was the best kisser they'd ever experienced.

When should you go in for the kiss?

The answer is, not immediately. Hollywood shows a leading man just grabbing a woman, yanking her close to him, and planting a hard, open-mouthed smacker right on her lips.

Don't imitate that in real life, because it's too risky.

While it may "slip her off her feet" if you kiss her full-on before she's even thinking about it, you'll have the best success statistically if you take it slowly.

While you can certainly go in quickly and

forcefully on the lips of a chick who you're sure is aroused and horny, if she's not yet aroused then you need to work up the sexual interaction before you can kiss her on the lips.

One of the best preludes to sex you can be in with a woman is the standard "make out" position on a couch. The two of you are sitting together, you with your arm resting behind her on the back cushions.

Let some time pass.

Then at some point, lightly touch her shoulder with your hand and then pull it back. Awhile later, put your hand more firmly on her shoulder. If she's interested in you, she'll snuggle up with you.

If she doesn't snuggle up, don't allow yourself to feel upset.

Instead relax and be cool. Just pull your arm back so that it's no longer touching her (but is still behind her on the top of the couch) and then try again later. Eventually, her horniness will have reached the point where she's dying to have your arm around her.

Put your arm around her.

Do various things that the two of you have done thus far. Hold hands. Snuggle. Run your fingers through her silky hair.

In fact, keep in mind the following parts of

her body that... although they're "Rated PG"... are in reality erogenous zones:

- **Her Hair.** Absolutely the best way to heat a woman up is to touch her hair.
- Touch her **scalp** as well, since that's erogenous.
- **The inside of her elbows.** The touch of your fingertips might make her shiver.
- **The skin between her fingers.** When you hold hands with a woman, the best way to do it is to interlock fingers with hers.
- **Her ears.** As you're getting close to kissing her, lightly blow into her ears. Touch the rims of her ears and her earlobes with your fingertips.
- **Her shoulders.**
- **Her feet.**
- **Her toes.**

Touch the above areas, and she'll get increasingly aroused.

As things get more and more heated, move your face toward her hair and inhale deeply. Say, "Mmmmm I love the way your hair smells!"

Do the same thing with the nape of her neck.

For some reason, sniffing a woman's hair and nape of her neck seems to have a powerful effect on almost every woman. Perhaps this is a primal instinct going back into our evolutionary history.

By the way, don't verbalize anything with the woman. Feminist propaganda notwithstanding, you will destroy the mood if you say stuff like, "Can I put your arm around you now?"

How to Move in For the Kiss The First Time

When it comes time for your first kiss with a new girlfriend, you can indirectly mention it, using what I like to call the "Rate Your Kiss" Technique.

Here's how the "Rate Your Kiss" Technique works. When you feel like the mood is right for the kiss, you say, "How would you rate your kissing ability on a scale of 1 to 10?"

She may answer or she may not, but at that point 95+% of the time the woman will open her lips and you can move your face towards hers.

Other than that technique, there is a big non-verbal signal to look for that says, "Kiss me now, my dream man!"

The technique in a nutshell is this...

As you move your face and lips very close to hers (after having already inhaled the scent of her hair and so on), watch for her to slightly part her lips and have them go soft. Usually a woman will also close her eyes, though not always.

By the way, do this with your steady girlfriend/wife too, not just with a girl you're having sex with for the first time.

When you move in, concentrate not on kissing her, but on brushing your lips against hers. Trust me, she'll melt into you and the two of you will be kissing full-on in no time.

Kiss for awhile, slowly. Have your mouth open. Wait for her tongue. Once the tip of her tongue enters your mouth, match what she does.

The Most Important Thing for You to Know About Kissing

Kissing differs from many other sexual activities in that it's one of the few things that you do with a woman in which you should let her take the lead. When it comes to activities such as eating her out and penetrating her, you should take the lead. But again, not with kissing.

One of the biggest mood-killers for a woman is when a guy jams his tongue into her mouth before she's ready. So just relax during the kissing and mirror what she does.

The Proper Mindset of the Master Kisser

Like so many other aspects of sexual intercourse, much of your success flows from your mindset. Don't be thinking about the bills you have to pay or the movie that's playing on the VCR while the two of you are making out on the couch.

Instead concentrate only on her mouth and the kissing. Let your mind go blank, as if you were entering a meditative state. The only thing that should be in your mind are the vision, feeling, smells, and tastes of that beautiful, soft, warm mouth of hers, and the sounds of her faint moans of pleasure.

Women have more sensitive bodily nerve endings that we do, plus they tend to feel emotions more strongly that we do. So whatever pleasure you feel will sweep even more powerfully over your partner. She will surge with tingly excitement as she loses strength in her body and her panties become soaked.

Techniques of a Make-Out Master

After kissing her on her lips for a bit, pull away and kiss other spots:
- Her cheeks.
- Her chin.
- Her jaw.

- The tip of her nose.
- Her forehead.
- Her ears. (Blow your hot breath softly into her ear, run your lips on the rim of her ear, and flick your tongue on her earlobes.)
- Her neck, moving down to the nape of her neck, her shoulders, and the top of her upper chest. (Don't attempt to kiss her breasts or do anything else with them yet. Merely going down to the top of her upper chest and then pulling back up will plant the proper seed in your woman's mind.)

Then move back up to her lips and kiss her passionately and deeply.

As she moves deeper into your mouth with her tongue, move yours deeper into hers as well. Taste her wonderful mouth.

Run your tongue along her teeth. Imagine that your tongue and hers are dance partners, doing a slow, sensual dance together.

It's good to have a lot of variety with the way you kiss a woman. Although the main course is open-mouth, you can add in some various side dishes.

One of my favorites is the closed-mouth mini-kiss. To do it, you hold your lips sealed against the woman's skin, then suck in a little bit of air into your mouth to create a little "smack smack smack."

Another good side dish is to simply kiss other parts of your woman's face and body. What I like to do is explore her body (avoiding her X-rated body parts early on) with my kisses. That means her neck, her arms, her legs, forehead, etc.

Always make her lips the center of your kissing, however. By that I mean, kiss her neck for awhile, then return to her lips. Kiss her nose and up to her eyebrows and forehead, then return to her lips. And so on.

Remember that, because it is only one part of the overall sexual intercourse, kissing should not be done by itself. While you're kissing your woman, you should also be caressing her all over. And then later when you're having intercourse with her, you should be kissing her throughout.

As a matter of fact, one of the great benefits of kissing is that it distracts the woman's mind. When you go in and touch her breasts for the first time, you should be passionately kissing her to reduce the likelihood of hearing those dreaded words, "not yet." Same thing when you go to touch her pussy for the first time. Et cetera.

The final thing to keep in mind about kissing your woman on the mouth is that you should almost always have your eyes closed when you do it. I know it's tempting to open your eyes and take in the beautiful sight of your woman's face so close to yours, but fight that temptation.

Women often get creeped out when they open their eyes during a kiss and see a couple wide-open eyes glaring right at them.

So when you kiss your woman on her lips, turn off your sense of sight and instead focus on your senses of touch, smell, and taste.

Be Proud of Your Body

If you're like most guys buying this book, you want to learn everything you can about how to make a woman's body feel good. You want to know her body up and down.

But to be a truly great lover, you need to also understand your own body.

In fact, in many ways it's more important for you to understand your own body and its sensations than it is to understand hers.

And not to be too shocking, but let's face it. As a great lover, your sexual power comes from... your penis.

The penis is the center of your pleasure, so it's time to truly allow it to be a part of you. For a lot of guys, its almost as if their dick is a third party during the sex.

Ever thought stuff to yourself like, "Geez, I should be thinking with my head, not with my dick."? Don't think such thoughts. Instead you should be one with your penis. It doesn't have a mind of its own.

It's time to become comfortable - truly comfortable - with your penis. Stop caring about its size. Whatever size it is, that's fine.

Because the bottom line with women is that they tend to believe whatever you believe about yourself:

If you're a confident man, then they'll think you're an attractive, alpha male sort of guy. If you have a strong opinion about what movie you want to go see, they'll go along with you. (Ever wondered why women find it attractive when a guy has a place in mind rather than just saying "Where would you like to go?" It's because they admire a man with strong beliefs.)

It's the same thing when it comes to your dick. If you're proud of it and completely love it, then your woman will as well.

And by the way, stop giving your dick a nickname, if you're one of those guys who do that. Your penis is a part of **you**... it's not some separate entity.

As a man, your power in bed comes from your penis. Get in tune with it and its sensations, and you can play your woman like your favorite musician plays the guitar.

Remember when you were a teenager and all the intricate parts of your penis and testicles fascinated you? It should be the same thing, if not more so, for you today.

No more being ashamed or self-conscious when it comes to your cock. Be grateful for it and pleased with it.

The benefits of your new attitude towards your penis will be enormous. As stated previously, you will you have the power to move a woman's entire world with the magnificence of your cock.

Also, a large factor that causes performance anxiety will be gone. A lot of men live in fear of their dicks, thinking things like, "Oh my God, I hope I can get it up tonight!"

The bottom line is that having sex is no different from breathing.

You don't worry about your lungs not working, so neither should you worry about your penis not filling with blood. You can get the same sexual pleasure with a flaccid penis than you can with a full erection.

A full erection isn't even required for you to have an orgasm. So stop worrying! You have nothing at all to fear.

Feel free to experiment all you want with your penis, and explore all new types of sensations with it.

So become fascinated once again with your glorious dick, and enjoy all of the good sensations that your body feels because of it.

How to Receive The Best Oral Possible

The feeling of a hot, wet, soft mouth sucking on your hungry penis is one of the best sensations you will ever experience. As a general rule, in order to get a woman to the point where she will happily give you these sensations, she must feel
- **Relaxed.**
- **Comfortable.**
- **Emotionally connected with you.**

Of course it is often the case that a woman will give you a blow-job as a "consolation prize" in lieu of vaginal intercourse, but to maximize your chances of getting a blowjob, you need to create those three feelings within your lover-girl.

If the woman starts the process of taking your dick into her mouth, the emotional connection is practically a given. Why? Because you are at your most vulnerable when her teeth are around your dick. So you are trusting her in an enormous way.

Getting her to feel comfortable and relaxed is the more challenging part. It is challenging because it requires you to control a massive urge that you've had your entire life, ever since you learned to masturbate.

What is that urge, you ask? It is the urge to be active when it comes to the sexual pleasure you receive.

Because of the urge to be active, the average man wants to grab his woman's head and start thrusting. Don't do it!

Instead, **remain passive** during the blowjob. Allow your woman to control the action. Lock your hands together behind your head and just lay back and relax.

If you feel the urge to touch her, then instead lightly stroke her neck and run your fingers through her hair.

Do not physically move her head, however, because women find this unpleasant and you don't want her to associate any unpleasantness whatsoever to the act of fellatio.

A woman who feels like she controls the tempo will have a higher comfort level. Try sticking a sausage in your mouth and you'll see why this is important. It's easy to start gagging, which is an unpleasant sensation.

So allow the woman to be in charge of the fellatio and let her choose the ways she will give pleasure to your dick.

Women tend to be highly self-conscious in the bedroom, and as a consequence she doesn't want to bite you or otherwise do a poor job and embarrass herself.

This brings up another point - societal conditioning. Women are taught from constant cultural barrages, media influence, societal gossiping from their friends, and religious messages that enjoyment of sex is "bad." This is the reason a lot of women turn cold on enjoying fellatio.

The solution? Praise, praise, and praise again! Let her know how much you enjoy the blowjob, both during it and afterwards.

Reward her good behavior by telling her how much you enjoyed it and are enjoying it. Examples:
- "I love the way you stroke my dick so tenderly."
- "Your mouth feels so good."
- "When you swallow, I feel so connected with you." (More on this in the next chapter.)
- "Ahhh yeah!" (Moan approvingly when you feel good.)
- "Baby, you are the best!"

Notice something that all of these have in common? They're all very simple. There's no need to recite Shakespearean Sonnets when receiving a blowjob.

In fact, women respond better when you lose control of yourself, feeling such intense pleasure that you tap into your most primal, lustful thoughts and become almost inarticulate.

So let yourself go, and be vocal when you feel her hot, moist tongue on the head of your dick.

Women feel a deep connection with you when they take your cock into their mouths and make you feel good. Have you ever noticed how even in porn films when the actresses are performing fellatio, they'll look into the man's eyes whenever they can?

Your woman will most likely do this too. When she does, return her gaze.

She is not just making any man feel good; she is making *you* feel good. She is not just tasting any man intimately; she's tasting you intimately.

Enjoy the view by pulling her hair away from her face. Not only do you get the visual stimulation of seeing your penis in a woman's mouth, but you also get the following two benefits:
1. It increases the tenderness between the two of you, merely by virtue of you having her silky hair intertwined in your fingers.
2. Women don't like when their hair gets in their eyes, nose, and mouth, so you are helping her do something she'd want to do anyway. This frees both her hands to massage your balls and ass and to stroke your dick up and

down.

You also need to have your dick be enticing to her. Keep the hair at the base of your penis shaved. And closely trim (or shave off entirely) the muff of pubic hair on your lower abdomen. This will greatly reduce the amount of hair that your woman gets in her mouth during the blowjob.

It will also give your genital area a clean appearance. You know how a woman's pussy looks a lot more enticing when it's shaved rather than having the appearance of a jungle? It's the same with our penises.

A side benefit to getting rid of all that long pubic hair is that it will reveal the entire length of your organ and make it appear longer.

Finally, it is very important keep your dick clean, because the combination of residual urine and sweat can make your crotch area smell noxious.

Use soap, but only very sparingly, and rinse thoroughly. You don't want the scent of the soap to clash with the natural aroma of pheromones that your genitals give off.

If you are uncircumcised, an oily fluid gathers under your foreskin and needs to be cleaned out from time to time. To do this, simply pull back the foreskin when you're in the shower and wash away the accumulated fluid.

How to Get Her to Swallow

When you come in a woman's mouth, you are giving her an awesome gift. Again, however, societal conditioning is a key reason a lot of women don't swallow. (For example, they hear from their friends that sperm is "icky" and that women who swallow are "sluts.")

So when your woman does swallow, give her **praise, praise, and more praise**. Tell her you like it when she swallows.

After she swallows, she'll want to kiss you on the lips. Allow her to. It's very important. Don't worry about getting your sperm in your mouth, because she will have swallowed it all, and you won't taste a thing.

Under no circumstances should you indicate that you think your own sperm is gross, nor should you be reluctant to kiss her on the lips. Women tend to be very deferential in their beliefs. If you believe your semen is gross, then she too will think that. But if you think it's normal and no big deal, then she too will think that.

As she becomes accustomed to the taste, your woman will grow to enjoy it. Studies have shown that humans enjoy the taste of flavors that they are exposed to on a consistent basis, and it doesn't matter whether they didn't like those flavors at first.

On an average western diet (i.e., pretty unhealthy), the typical man has semen that taste salty and bitter, with a pH of above 8, comparable to an egg white.

Particularly in men whose diets are high in dairy, the texture often is reported to be an unpleasant clumpiness, leaving an aftertaste.

The good news, however, is **"you come what you eat."** Through improved diet, you can improve the taste and texture of your semen enough to make your girlfriend enjoy swallowing.

In order to make your semen taste as good as possible, you need to maximize your intake of the foods and liquids that have been experimented with and shown to improve it.

What to consume:

1. **Pineapple juice.** You should make it a ritual to have one glass of pineapple juice everyday. Out of everything, this is the number one thing you can consume to make your come taste better.

2. **Cinnamon.** (Try a teaspoon a day.)... the #1 taste-improving spice you can consume and overall is 2nd only to pineapple juice in the immediate improvement it makes to semen taste. The best way to take cinnamon is to mix

it with oatmeal for your breakfast. Oatmeal is one of the best foods you can eat as a weightlifter because it has complex, slow-to-digest carbs and has a good amount of protein. (And by the way, in order to boost your testosterone levels, you need to start lifting weights. But we'll get to that later.)

3. Other semen-improving spices are **nutmeg** and **ginger**. (An easy way to consume these spices is to simply add them to your oatmeal.)

4. Lots of **water**. H2O reduces semen saltiness and improves texture. (A common complaint of women who spit out cum is that they don't like its texture.)

5. **Fresh fruit** such as strawberries, bananas, grapes, papayas, mangoes, and of course pineapple.

6. **Citrus fruit** full of acid, such as oranges.

7. **Sweet melons** such as cantaloupe and watermelon.

8. **Vegetables,** particularly celery, broccoli, and avocados.

9. Non-sugar sweeteners, especially **Splenda**. They are more concentrated in their sweetness than sugar and will not be resisted by your body's insulin the way sugar will be.

What to avoid:

1. **Tobacco** in any quantity.

2. **Asparagus** in any quantity.

3. **Beets.**

4. **Beer.**

5. **Excessive red meat.** Too much can make your semen too alkaline and affect its smell.

6. Excessive quantities of **strong-tasting fish**.

7. **Fried starches** such as potato chips.

8. **Excessive amounts of bread.** This can give semen a bad texture.

9. **Garlic.**

10. **Raw onions.**

11. **Cabbage.**

12. **Dairy products in excessive amounts.**

13. **Excessive salt.**

14. **Coffee.**

   Basically, when it comes to eating, you can adjust the flavor of your come based on saltiness, sweetness, sour, and degree of bitterness.

What makes pineapple so ideal is that it's highly sweet and acidic. The acid reduces the alkalinity of your semen, making it less bitter.

Foods being on the "avoid" list doesn't necessarily mean that you should never partake in them.

Red meat is a good source of zinc, which helps with sperm and testosterone production. If you're a bodybuilder, red meat and dairy products can be a great source of the protein you need to build muscle. Just make sure not to go overboard with them, and to drink your pineapple juice daily.

One basic rule for many of the foods on the avoid list is the question, "Do they affect my urine?" Just as asparagus and coffee influence the smell of your urine, so too do they influence your semen.

It takes a minimum of 12 hours from the time you eat semen-friendly foods to the time they start to have an effect on taste, so plan accordingly.

An easy way to consume large quantities of fruits quickly and easily is through the use of a juicer.

Having tried different brands of juicers, the kind I recommend is the Champion Juicer (which you can find through doing a Google search) because, as a "masticating" juicer, it grinds up the fruit in such a way that the juice maintains its full amount of vitamins. Cheaper juicers that spin the fruit tend to aerate the juice, which depletes it of a lot of the vitamins.

It should be noted that semen itself is healthy for a woman to consume. The average amount of ejaculate (one teaspoon) contains 5-7 calories and has important vitamins and minerals your woman needs like Vitamin C, iron, and zinc.

Another thing for you to watch is where you aim the come that you shoot into your woman's mouth. When you're pumping your dick into a hot, hungry vagina, you have to urge to push your dick in as far as it will go just before you come. This is a biological reflex because it ensures that the woman's uterus will be bathed in the maximum amount of life-giving sperm.

When you're coming in your woman's mouth and pump and shoot as deep as possible, however, you can trigger her involuntary gag reflex, which will cause her to associate unpleasant feelings with having you come in her mouth.

To avoid this, pull your dick out so that only the head is in her mouth when you ejaculate. Try to aim so that your semen hits the roof or sides of her mouth rather than the back of her throat.

Another option is to simply have your woman suck your penis while you're lying down. That way she'll be in control of how far your penis goes into her mouth when you orgasm.

Sometimes you may encounter a woman who's had negative experiences with fallatio in the past and is simply afraid to swallow.

When this happens, have her suck on Tic Tacs or some other kind of breath mint just before sucking your dick. The strong flavor of the mint will mask the taste of your come.

Eventually as your woman realizes your come tastes good (since you will have been eating semen-friendly foods), she will swallow your load happily.

Try to give your woman some kind of warning before you orgasm. This can either be explicit, by saying "I'm gonna come!" or it can be implicit, by loudly moaning and even screaming out in pleasure as your orgasm becomes inevitable.

Because fallatio is based on a strong emotional connection between man and woman, you need to allow yourself to have a lot of visibly apparent facial expressions of pleasure. Now is not the time for a poker face!

As you gasp and shoot your streams of hot semen into your woman's mouth, look deeply into her eyes. The emotional effect on her will be extraordinary.

Let her know how much pleasure you get

from her sucking your cock and swallowing your come. If she focuses on the pleasure she's giving you, she will bestow you with the kind of blowjobs that rock your world.

Slowness is Important

As guys, we have a strong biological urge to come as quickly as possible.

This is because when we get horny, we're ready to **feel as good as we can**. How do we achieve this? By reaching orgasm. Once we're turned on, we're ready to go at maximum speed towards the goal.

Women are different. They slowly heat up. Sex for them is not about the orgasm... it's about the sex itself. If they orgasm, that's an added awesome bonus. If they don't orgasm, that's cool too.

So there's no need for a woman to go right for a quick orgasm. As a matter of fact, it often makes her feel like the sex was not as good as she could have been.

Instead take your time and slowly tease your woman. This will give you the additional benefit of overcoming any nervousness.

Here's a big secret that will instantly make you a far better lover.

Start viewing sex as a relaxation exercise rather than a vigorous workout.

Sex is not something you need to have energy for. Instead it's a way to unwind at the end of a long day, no different from getting a massage by the pool.

Once you make that simple change in the way you visualize sex, it will instantly take away all the performance pressure you have.

Plus no matter how tired you feel, you'll be able to make love to your woman. Sex does not have to be something that requires any effort at all.

Every Woman is Unique

No matter how good you become with any particular woman, never assume that those skills are directly transferable to any other woman.

If you're with a new woman and aren't sure what she likes, err on the side of caution. It's far better to have her aching for more than it is to kill her mood by being too forceful.

By the way, you can never go wrong by moving slower in bed than a woman wants. This just gets her more turned on.

The Key to Going Slow

If there's one key word you should be focusing on, it should be **"tease."** Think of yourself like a master chef, teasing the wonderful flavors out of a pot of food. You wouldn't just dig in when it's raw. Instead the best food comes from being cooked slowly, with just the right amount of spices, added at the perfect times.

(Once a woman has heated up, however, there's no need anymore to take your time. If a woman is completely comfortable with you and she has reached a high degree of horniness, she will practically grab your hand and move it to her clit. When your head is hovering near her pussy as a way to tease her, she will put her hands behind your head and jam it into her dripping cunt.)

So be soft and slow at first with your touches. Avoid her genitals.

Remember, women are the opposite of us. While we'd love for our dicks to be grabbed ASAP, you should wait to touch her clit, ass, and tits until she's sufficiently turned on.

This is because women are sensitive everywhere. So keep touching and kissing her entire body. Even when you're gotten to the point, later on, where you're paying attention to her clitoral area, still keep your hands busy on the rest of her body to keep compounding her pleasure.

Your purpose of all this gentle caressing is to create a desire within her. Although you desperately want to push your finger into her moist, hot hole, you must remain steadfast.

Touch her softly all over her body. Run your fingers so lightly over her skin that they're barely touching it.

This first phase can last as long as you want it to, but at a minimum you should take about five minutes.

At that point, you will have created a sensation within her of melting at your touch. She will be increasingly overcome by emotion and open to an escalation of your mating ritual.

Move your fingers in a zig zag pattern, taking your time and being lazy as you torture her with pleasure, towards her breasts. Circle them with your fingertips.

Then grab her breasts with your palms and fingers, but do not touch her nipples yet. Move your hands away and kiss her breasts to the left and right, above and below her nipples, but again not directly on them. Do this for at least three minutes.

The desire within her is increasing further. All she is thinking about is how badly she wants you to touch her aching nipples.

Now use your tongue. You can move to other parts of her body such as her stomach and belly button, in order to increase the sweet torture further. Kiss and lick her all around, again avoiding all the "X-rated" areas of her body.

Once you move back to her breasts with your licking, lick around her nipples but not directly on them. Continue to softly touch and caress her body at the same time.

Avoid going right for her nipples, because the average woman's nipples are very sensitive. What you should do is circle them, in a spiral drawing closer and closer to them.

Go lightly enough that she doesn't feel uncomfortable.

Note: how hard you should press down depends on the woman. However, as a general rule, the bigger a woman's natural breast size is, the less sensitive she feels there. (I say "natural" breast size because women with gel implants have the same sensitivity that they did when their boobs were unscarred by surgery.) Basically, every woman has the same number of nerve endings in her breasts, and those with smaller tits have the nerves more concentrated.

Watch for your woman's nipples to become more and more erect the closer you get.

Once her nipples have become accustomed to your touch, you can start to squeeze, adjusting for her comfort. This creates a high amount of pleasure in women.

Chicks I've been with have told me that

once I start sucking on their hard nipples, they can feel sensations throughout their body... even down to their pussy.

There's no need to spend a long time at a woman's nipples. Though it's possible for them to orgasm from nipple stimulation, you'll most likely want to move elsewhere.

Slowly, of course.

The key point of moving slow is that not only does she slowly heat up until she becomes an insatiable animal in heat, but it also **keeps you in control** of the whole interaction. This is big with women, especially during the early sexual encounters (but all throughout a relationship to be sure). Women want a man who is confident and in control.

It will be obvious to you from her signals that she's dying to have you move toward the next step. Her moaning may become louder, she may spread her legs extremely wide, she may touch your penis, etc.

Once you detect those signals, move the sexual interaction forward.

Your Health and Diet

What if I told you there was a miracle hormone that:

- Powers your sex drive (the most important goal of course!) by causing you to have increased sexual desires and fantasies?
- Helps you perform sexually by stimulating blood flow?
- Increases the volume of your semen?
- Increases the number of sperm that your body produces?
- Increases your ability to become erect, and causes your erections to be longer and thicker?
- Increases your pleasure from sex by boosting the sensations you feel in your penis?
- Increases the frequency that you can have sex... meaning that you can "get it up" again much sooner after you come?
- Makes your semen taste better to women because it induces your seminal vesicles to produce the sugar fructose?
- Builds muscles?
- Keeps your metabolism high?
- Possibly even helps you live longer by, among other things, keeping your heart healthy?

- Increases your happiness?
- Increases your masculine vigor?
- Is the most effective aphrodisiac?

That miracle hormone, and by far the most important male sex hormone, is, if you haven't figured it out yet... testosterone.

The biggest hormonal influence on your sex drive is testosterone. Testosterone is a hormone that powers your sex drive. Not only that, but it builds muscle.

Your body produces testosterone naturally. Here's how it works, in a nutshell... basically, the Leydig cells in your balls converts cholesterol into into testosterone, and then releases that miracle hormone into your bloodstream.

Every day, your body produces 4 to 10 MG of testosterone. And depending on how much sex you have, your body secretes 4 to 10 MG a day. (Every time you come inside your woman, you inject testosterone into her.)

So, in order to be able to have more sex, you need to have your body produce more testosterone.

This also has a feedback loop kind of effect... not only does having a higher amount of sex require you to produce more testosterone, but **the more testosterone you have floating around freely in your body, the higher your desire is for sex.**

So now you know the benefits of testosterone, and why you want your body to produce a massive amount of it.

But what about taking synthetic testosterone, i.e., steroids? That puts a lot of the good stuff in your bloodstream, right? Not so fast.

Ninety-five percent of the testosterone your body produces is made by your testicles. So when you take steroids, your balls literally shrink from lack of use.

Additionally, your body converts excess unneeded testosterone into estrogen. That's why guys at the gym who take too much steroids develop ghastly conditions like gynecomastia ("bitch tits").

So avoid steroids.

What you want to do instead is make sure your body produces ample testosterone on its own. This is done in two ways:
1. By eliminating the things you do that reduce your testosterone production.
2. By doing the things that have been proven to boost your testosterone production.

With that in mind, following these 21 guidelines will boost the amount of Miracle Hormone your body produces:

1. Give Up Butts.

You are literally killing your sex drive and punching yourself in the balls every time you you take a drag on a cigarette. Researchers have found that smokers have fewer of the cells in their testicles that produce testosterone... and the ones that were still alive were damaged.

Additionally, cigarettes reduce the amount of oxygen in your blood, which produces softer erections. The worst thing you could ever do as a man is interfere with your blood flow. Reduced blood flow directly translates into reduced sex.

The reason cigarette smoke reduces the oxygen in your blood is chiefly because of the carbon monoxide you absorb from it. Carbon monoxide molecules replace oxygen molecules in your blood.

And this not only means you have softer erections. Because all of the systems in your body get damaged by the carbon monoxide, this means you also have less energy for sex.

So if you smoke, the absolute best thing you can do for your sex life is to quit.

How do you quit? It's one of those things that's simple but not easy. The way to quit is to want to quit. It's impossible for me to know what would make you want to quit. You need to explore and decide that for yourself. That's the part that isn't easy, but it must be done.

For me, the motivation came when I began lifting weights and bodybuilding. I'd keep a journal of how much I lifted each week, always trying to life more every week. As a consequence, I'd do whatever it took to be able to life more weight. That desire within me outweighed my desire for nicotine.

Later on, I read in-depth about the harmful effects of smoking to the human body... and was astounded by the massive degree to which smoking is harmful. It's not an overstatement to say that smoking destroys every cell in your body... so smoking doesn't just mean you'll die at 70 years old instead of 80. It also means your quality of life is cut down the whole time.

2. Keep Your Jewels Cool.

Prolonged exposure of your balls to heat can literally cause your sperm cells to die from heat stroke.

The reason your nutsack hangs down off your body is that sperm thrives in an environment cooler than your body's regular temperature. The optimal temperature of your testicles is 95 degrees Fahrenheit. So avoid exposing them to temperatures higher than that.

Take showers instead of baths. Put your laptop computer on your desk instead of the top of your lap. Wear boxers instead of tighty whities.

3. Keep Sober to Keep Your Sperm

Watch out for excess alcohol consumed over a long period of time (AKA alcoholism). A lot of people who are alcoholics deny being so, but here's the point: a study conducted by the Duke University Medical Center concluded that drinking causes reduced ability to have erections, plus lower sperm count and semen production.

Even just having alcohol in your system disrupts your body's ability to have powerful orgasms.

I'm not saying you should become a teetotaler. Feel free to have a cold one from time to time with buddies, or some wine with your woman at dinner. Just be aware of the effect alcohol has on your sexual function and adjust the amount that you drink to take that into account.

As far as your body's production of testosterone is concerned, stopping chronic drinking is one of the quickest ways to boost the amount of this "miracle hormone" in your bloodstream.

In one study, researchers studied testosterone levels in men after they consumed alcohol. They found that becoming drunk can sink your testosterone levels by as much as

25%. Getting drunk also spikes the amount of estrogen in your system.

A second reason to avoid excessive alcohol is that it can block your body's absorption of many key nutrients. Three nutrients especially needed by your body for come production - calcium, magnesium, and zinc - are ravaged by excessive alcohol.

Thirdly, you need to stay well-hydrated in order to have energy for sex, good blood flow for the most solid erection possible, and to avoid having the clumpy-textured semen that many women don't like in their mouths. Unfortunately, alcohol dehydrates your muscle cells.

Finally (and this isn't directly sex-related), if you do decide to have a serious workout program, bear in mind that alcohol retards muscle growth. It reduces your body's ability to break down protein and help build muscle... by as much as 20%.

So the bottom line is this... if you're a chronic drinker, you're altering your body's metabolism of testosterone and even increasing the amount of estrogen it produces. So if you're an alcoholic, and sex is more important to you than drink, then get your ass to Alcoholics Anonymous.

4. Moderate Your Meds.

Many medications affect your body's

testosterone levels and/or reduce your sperm count. The worst offenders are anti-depressants, anti-anxiety drugs, ulcer medicine, and anti-inflammatories.

A key point about all of these medications is that a huge reason why guys take them is because they're actually suffering from symptoms of testosterone deficiency. So stop taking them, and work on living a healthy lifestyle, and you might find that your symptoms will go away.

If you have problems with depression or anxiety, a better option before resorting to medication is to work on controlling your emotional state. Take a realistic view of your life. Being depressed doesn't solve a thing, so suck it up and quit being down on yourself.

In large part, ulcers are caused by overeating, excess alcohol consumption, caffeine (which stimulates your stomach to secrete acid), smoking, and of course stress. So the best away to avoid them is to eat and drink moderately and take care of your health.

Avoid situations that cause you to feel angry. Also avoid dwelling on thoughts that make you angry. Simply not thinking about bad situations will reduce 90% of the anger you feel from them.

Avoid anti-inflammatories as much as possible, as they can reduce your sperm count and your ability to maintain solid erections.

These are the drugs like ibuprofen that you take for headaches, back pains, etc.

Most of the time anti-inflammatories only treat the symptoms, not the underlying illness. So if you have a headache, find out what the root cause of it is before you pop that Advil.

If your headache's caused by caffeine cravings, then work on eliminating coffee and cola from your diet.

Some additional miscellaneous sperm-killing medications to watch out for are:
- Cimetidine (sold under the brand name Tagamet).
- Nitrofurantoin.
- Sulfasalazine

This should go without saying, but also avoid illegal drugs such as marijuana and cocaine as they can lower your sperm count.

If your headache's caused by stress, then learn relaxation techniques. You can teach yourself to relax and not feel so stressed out. See below.

5. Just Relax.

This can be difficult for the average guy who lives in the go-go world of hustle and bustle. But adopt these strategies, and stress will no longer consume you:

Don't allow things to upset you if there's

nothing you can do about it.

Getting upset at that driver who's following you too closely won't cause him to back off. Veins popping in your forehead at the thought of that chick who rejected you won't help anything either. You can't control the way a woman thinks or behaves.

Make priorities in life. Work towards your priorities all the time and be focused only on them.

I learned this from a friend who got started in the import-export business and became successful. His goals were to build a solid company and become wealthy. So anything that was different from that literally was "the small stuff" that he couldn't care less about.

Make things happen rather than getting upset and complaining.

Sure, it may be tempting to feel pissed off about all the leaves in your front yard, but just grab a god damn rake and get to work on it (or hire someone else to do it), and the problem will be solved.

6. Have More Sex to Have More Testosterone.

Lack of sex can be a testosterone killer. Basically, "use it or lose it" applies to your dick and balls just as it applies to many other things in your life.

If you don't have a regular sex partner, masturbate. Try to ejaculate at least once every two days, so that your testicles are constantly producing new semen and testosterone.

However, don't masturbate so much that you sexually satisfy yourself. You want to find sexual release from women, not your hand.

By the way, there's a common myth that sex and/or masturbation reduce testosterone.

The truth of the matter is this... every time you ejaculate, you've shot some testosterone out of your body, so for a few hours thereafter your testosterone levels will be lower than they were before you came. However, in the long run, when your body produces new testosterone, it will produce more than before.

As a matter of fact, studies have shown that men with low testosterone levels are more irritable and agitated than men with normal levels. So that may be why men who get laid a lot tend to be more mellow and laid back than men who don't.

7. Lose the Spare Tire.

A bit of body fat is good, but if you're so overweight that your insulin levels have become elevated, that blocks your body from producing a particular type of protein that's crucial to testosterone circulation in your bloodstream.

A couple added benefits to losing the excess blubber are that your dick appears longer without all that fat around it and you look more attractive to women overall. (High bodyfat is a feminine, not masculine, trait.)

Particularly onerous is belly fat. A study of middle-aged men revealed that there's an inverse correlation between the amount of fat in your belly and the amount of testosterone in your bloodsteam. So even if you're thin except for a spare tire around the middle, it is still critical that you lose the fat.

8. Don't be Too Skinny.

Your body uses fat to produce testosterone, so if the level of fat becomes too low in your body, you have less of this precious hormone.

Make sure to consume the right kind of fat... the omega 3s and other fats that contain HDL or "good cholesterol." Flaxseed oil, olive oil, and fatty fishes are good sources of these essential fats.

9. Eat Less Estrogen.

Estrogens in your diet come from sources you'd never suspect.

One of the biggest offenders is soy. It contains estrogen-like chemicals that can boost your body's supply of that hormone. (In fact, a large reason that post-menopausal women consume soy is that it acts in many ways as estrogen replacement therapy!)

Another source of estrogen is from conventional store-bought poultry. In order to grow chickens as fast as possible, to produce that plump white chicken meat that consumers crave so much, the feed given to chickens on factory farms is full of estrogen.

So instead of buying conventional chicken, pay the extra money to buy "hormone free" or even organic chickens.

10. Yes, You Can Eat Cholesterol.

Not all cholesterol is bad. Consume more of the "good cholesterol" (HDL) and less of the "bad cholesterol" (LDL). Researchers have found that men with high levels of HDL have higher testosterone.

Avoid consuming too many saturated fats. Also, avoid trans fats in any quantities. Look for "partially hydrogenated oil" and "vegetable shortening" in ingredients labels. The main offenders are margarine and packaged baked goods like cookies and crackers.

You can find the good fats in...
- Fatty cold-water fish such as salmon.
- Flaxseed oil (which you can find at organic food stores).
- Nuts.

Also consume more fiber, which reduces your LDL levels.

11. Cut Carbs.

A diet high simple sugars and starches can create your blood levels of cortisol and insulin to spike. These two hormones harm your body's production of testosterone.

Foods to avoid are:
* Breads, particularly low-fiber white bread.
* Pasta.
* Potatoes.

12. Fruits and Vegetables Jump Start Your Sex Life

Eat as much fruits and vegetables as you can. An ideal quantity in your diet is about 70%.

This isn't as hard as it sounds... if you drop the refined carbs such as white bread from your diet (which should be dropped... see the chapter on "How to Get Her to Swallow"), then you can easily find yourself eating 30% meat and 70% fruits and vegetables.

Don't worry about it if you can't attain that high of a level, however. A study in the US showed that adding just one piece of fruit and one serving of vegetables to your daily diet can increase your testosterone considerably.

Every time you ejaculate, you lose the

following nutrients: Vitamins B6, B12, and E; Calcium; Chlorophyll; Magnesium; Selenium; and Zinc.

As you replenish your body's stocks of these nutrients, you'll also notice an increase in the volume of your semen.

Foods rich in some or all of these semen-replenishing nutrients are:
- Oysters. (Yes, the rumors about the benefits of this food are true.)
- Beef.
- Nuts, especially cashews, pecans, and walnuts.
- Oatmeal.
- Whole wheat bread.
- Avocados.

It's also important to get lots of vitamin C... good semen-friendly sources of which being pineapple juice and oranges. Studies have shown that the more Vitamin C you consume as part of your daily diet, the higher your sperm count is.

Spotlight on the power vegetables that will boost your masculinity:

Eat more cruciferous vegetables. Studies have shown that these vegetables boost your testosterone more than any other, due to them being rich in a particular chemical called indole-3-carbinol, which turns the testosterone-suppressing estrogens in your body into ones that boost your body's production of the Miracle

Hormone.

What are cruciferous vegetables? These are:
- Broccoli.
- Brussels sprouts.
- Cabbage.
- Collard greens.
- Cress.
- Kale.
- Kohlrabi.
- Mustard greens.
- Radishes.
- Turnip greens.
- Watercress.

You don't like any of these vegetables, you say? Try raw broccoli with soft cheese spread on it. The soft cheese drowns out the nasty taste of the broccoli. And remember that by eating that wonderful snack, you're boosting your testosterone and improving the taste of your semen, which kills two birds with one stone.

Something else I recommend is wheatgrass juice. Wheatgrass has been popular in Eastern traditions for awhile. Recently, University of San Diego researchers found a compound in this plant that increases your production of sperm.

13. Increase Your Bulk Rate

Work out with weights and eat more protein. When you lift weights, testosterone levels in your blood can go up by over 30%. Eating enough protein will give your body the raw material pack on the muscle

The best workouts are those in which you work multiple sets rather than just lift for a single set. The best exercises are compound exercises such as squats and deadlifts that work your large muscle groups and many of them at a time.

As a general rule, the more difficult the exercise (meaning the more weight you lift), the greater the testosterone boost you'll get. Focus on high intensity... do high weights for a low number of reps, rather than low weights for a high number of reps.

Following your workout, you can increase the amount of testosterone in your system by consuming a protein shake with the right amount carbohydrates. I recommend having whey protein mixed with milk. They best kind for the price is ON Whey, which you can order cheaply and reliably from bodybuilding.com.

14. Get Fit Fast

Any exercise that makes you breathe hard - not just weightlifting - that you do to exhaustion kicks your body into testosterone-making high gear. Additionally, exercising on a regular basis keeps your level of testosterone elevated over the long term.

Aerobic workouts like jogging or working

out with a punching bag boost the amount of oxygen in your bloodstream and improve the flow of blood in your body. Not only does this make it easier for you to have erections (and makes them more powerful), but aerobic exercise has also been found to improve the quality of your sperm.

Avoid overdoing exercise, however. (This goes for both cardio and weight training.) Extreme exercising like training for a marathon can cause your testosterone to drop by up to 40%.

This is because when you overtrain, your body produces the hormone coritsol. This is the same testosterone-killing hormone produced when you're stressed out.

15. Win

Engage in competitions in areas that you're good at. Studies have shown that, believe it or not, winning at something can boost your testosterone levels. Losing can cause your testosterone levels to go down.

And it literally doesn't matter what you do. Top football players have been found to have higher testosterone than normal, but so have top mathematicians.

By the way, being good at something will also boost your confidence level, which makes you more attractive to women.

16. Control Your Caffeine

There have been a lot of studies done on caffeine, and the majority have shown the drug to be detrimental to your testicles.

For example, a study in Denmark of couples drinking from 3 to 7 cups of coffee a day found that the man's ability to impregnate his woman fell by a third, due to much their sperm being in twisted shapes and dead.

(I'm not saying that you should necessarily want to get your woman pregnant, by the way. But the best way to avoid pregnancy is by using birth control, not by damaging your body's production of sperm.)

Studies have shown that consuming caffeine on a regular basis decreases your body's production of testosterone. Most likely this is because caffeine screws with your adrenal glands.

Caffeine also makes it hard for you to relax because it makes you jittery. To have the best possible sex, you need to be relaxed.

To add to this laundry list about caffeine, it depletes your body of many of the vitamins it needs to produce ample semen and testosterone, such as the B vitamins, vitamin C, calcium, and zinc.

Finally, caffeine constricts your blood vessels, which inhibits your penis from filling up with blood and getting the powerful erections that make you a good lover.

17. Drink More Water

In order for glands such as your testicles to run at full capacity, you need to be fully hydrated. When your body becomes dehydrated, your glands are some of the first bodily functions to be shut down until you can replenish your fluids.

In other words, the less water you drink, the less testosterone your body produces. So try to have a bottle of water with yourself at all times throughout the day and then next to your bed at night. Get in the habit of constantly taking sips.

18. Eat Like a Caveman

Studies have shown that eating more meat induces your body to produce more testosterone. Avoid a lot of saturated fat like you find in pork and try to stick with...
Lean beef. (Look for cuts with the word "round" in the label such as top round and bottom round. Sirloin is also good.)
Hormone-free chicken.
Fish.

19. Sleep Well

Get a full night's sleep, every night. If you become sleep deprived, your testosterone levels plummet.

What's important is getting Rapid Eye Movement (REM) sleep. This occurs an average of 90 minutes after you doze off.

So even if you get prevented from having a full eight hours of sleep overnight, you can still take power naps of two hours or so to give your testosterone a boost.

So it's not an overstatement to say that sleep is like weightlifting for your penis.

During every REM phase, you get an erection as your glands work on releasing more testosterone into your system. (If you've ever wondered why you get erections at night, that's why.) This happens about five times a night.

So get as comfortable as possible at night so your sleep isn't interrupted. Remember: eight hours of sleep makes your dick stronger.

Just like when you hit the weights at the gym, the basic philosophy that in-shape guys have is, use it lose it. Well, it's the same thing when it comes to your dick and getting enough sleep: use it or lose it. Get enough sleep, or lose your penis power.

20. Turn Off the Cell

Your cellphone is bad for your balls.

A university study in Hungary found that

men who carry mobile telephones in their hip pockets had a sperm count 30% lower than other men.

Though the studies are not yet definitive (for example, one critique of the study suggests that perhaps men who carry cells in their pocket simply have more stress than other guys)... I highly suggest erring on the side of caution by keeping your cell phone away from your balls.

When you do have to carry your phone in your pocket, make sure it's turned off.

21. Sunbathe

Have you ever read about seasonal affective disorder (SAD)? It's the label psychologists give to the phenomenon of increased levels of depression in the population during winter time, which is caused by a lack of exposure to sunlight when people stay inside all day during cold spells.

The cure for SAD is either exposure to sunlight or treatment with bright lights.

Studies of men who underwent the same bright-light therapy that SAD sufferers receive shows that such therapy excites a man's pituitary gland, causing him to have a rise in his testosterone levels.

Try to get sunlight particularly in the early morning, which the studies showed to be the best time of day to get the exposure. You can kill two birds with one stone by jogging outside in shorts and short sleeves on your cardio workout days. (Even if it's cold outside, you'll warm up soon enough during your jog.)

22. Meditate

Do you think meditation is for pussies? Well, studies have found that guys who practice techniques in stress relief have higher levels of testosterone.

The reason stress relief works is that it lowers your boy's levels of testosterone-killing cortisol.

Some exercises involving meditation are yoga and Tai Chi. An added bonus of yoga in particular is that overwhelming numbers of its practitioners are women. In the yoga classes I've taken over the years, I've usually been the only straight guy in a room full of hot, sexy women. Definitely a nice situation to be in!

Yoga and meditation will teach you how to clear all the cobwebs from your mind and set you at ease. Not only that, but you'll learn proper postures and methods of breathing, keeping you more mellowed out in general.

Six Aphrodisiacs That Really Work

Imagine if you could kick your woman's sexual desire into overdrive simply by feeding her. Well, you can!

Certain foods have been reputed to have aphrodisiacal qualities going all the back to ancient Egypt 5,000 years ago. And the evidence says they work!

So next time you're feeding your woman, make her wet for you by giving her these...

Oysters

This is probably the #1 aphrodisiac there is, bar none.

Oysters have a reputation going back to ancient Rome, and were devoured by Casanova, who is said to have eaten 50 oysters a day to maintain his stamina to satisfy the 122 women he seduced.

And so it would have remained... as just an old wives tale... until in March 2005, a study came out that revealed the amazing secret of this wonderful mollusk.

At the risk of getting too technical,

researchers found two rare amino acids in oysters, called D-aspartic acid and N-methyl-D-aspartate.

These are two amino acids that trigger production of progesterone in women, making them horny. (Incidentally, these two amino acids also trigger testosterone production in men.)

Don't like oysters? Mussels and clams have them too.

Whatever your preference, however, eat them raw. Cooking destroys the two amino acids.

Chocolate

The magic ingredient is cocoa, which contains a chemical phenylethylamine (PEA), which is the same chemical released by your brain when you are in love.

When buying chocolate, find some that's high in cocoa... a good source is the typical natural foods store such as Earthfare or Whole Foods.

Cinnamon

Boosts the blood flow and is traditionally considered to be an aphrodisiac.

Cloves

Another traditional aphrodisiac, although there's no medical evidence for such. However, in my own testing of cooking chicken with cloves and chicken without cloves for women, I've found that women tend to be hornier after eating the latter.

Honey

This sticky, sweet substance is full of amino acids and B vitamins. Instead of licking whipped cream off of each other, use honey.

Nutmeg

This spice has been used for centuries as an aphrodisiac in China, India, and the Middle East.

Nutmeg only works as an aphrodisiac in small doses, however. This is because it contains a hallucinogenic drug called mescaline.

So a person should not consume more than a teaspoon, unless they prefer getting high to having sex. (Don't know about you, but I prefer sex.)

The very best appetizer you can feed a woman, I have found... in fact, it's almost like waving a magic wand on a chick to cast a horniness spell... is a plate of raw oysters sprinkled with nutmeg.

If a woman doesn't like oysters, you can make a game out of eating it. Laugh and joke with her about how gross they look, and then dare her to swallow one, etc.

A Woman's Anatomy

Since the pussy will become the object of your deepest affection, you need to know just what it is you worship.

You can think of the pussy as having two parts: the inside and the outside. The outside of the pussy is called the vulva.

If you examine her vulva, you see that she multiple lips. These lips are called the labia. The large outer lips are the labia majora or outer labia, while the delicate inner lips are called the labia minora or simply the inner labia.

At the top of her slit, inside her inner labia, you'll find her clitoris, which is covered by a clitoral hood. (Usually the clitoral hood covers the clit, except when she gets sexually excited and the clit becomes engorged, pushing through the clitoral hood.)

Moving down her slit from the clitoris, you'll find her urethra, which is where her urine comes out (not from her vagina... so contrary to what you might have believed, women actually have three holes down there, not two.)

Moving down further, you'll find the vagina, which of course is the love tunnel into which you'll insert your penis.

Below the vagina, you'll find her perineum, the mass of muscle and nerve tissue between her vagina and anus, which can be massaged (and feels good) in women just as it does when guys' perineums get a woman's special treatment.

Overcoming Sexual Anxiety

It is said that the largest sex organ in the body is the brain. Sexual arousal is more psychological than it is physical.

Sexual anxiety can occur when your psychology goes haywire. You try to do a good job at sex, which causes you to feel worried that you won't. Your worry interferes with your ability to have a solid erection. This makes you even more worried the next time you have sex, which makes it that much harder to have sex (and so on).

You need, therefore, to change your thinking and break out of that vicious cycle. I'll come back to how to do that.

Things can also be tough if you're new to having sex. When I first started out with my first girlfriend, I didn't know where her vagina was!

Human nature is to feel scared when you're doing something you've never done before. It's a normal psychological reaction. Even kissing a girl can be scary when you're inexperienced, because you're not sure that you're doing it right. It's not like they teach those things in school.

That's where this guide will help you. You

will be armed with the knowledge that you need to be her best lover ever, so you need not fear. Simply knowing and applying the chapter entitled "Slowness is Important" will separate you from 95% of guys.

Anxiety due to being new to sex is the best kind of anxiety to have. Why? Because the cure is simple: just have sex!

So let's get back to the other type of anxiety, which is due to issues of self-esteem. By this I mean that even though you've had sex in the past and are familiar with how the process works, you're obsessing over what the girl thinks of you and whether you'll perform sufficiently to satisfy her.

The solution is shocking, but it is effective. What is the solution? It is to adopt this affirmation...

"I couldn't care less what she thinks."

An affirmation is a statement to yourself that you repeat constantly. As you repeat it to yourself, visual yourself as the type of guy who "couldn't care less what she thinks." Feel the pleasure that you'll have in the bedroom when you're freed from such constraints.

Of course if you're in a good relationship, you will still care what she thinks and not act like a jerk. However, by doing your affirmation, you'll moderate your beliefs into something that's more healthy.

Because let's face it, you have no control over your woman. You can only control your own sexual pleasure.

When you adopt this "I don't care what she thinks" attitude in the bedroom, you create a mindset within yourself of non-attachment.

You see, the more you stress about sex, the more you sabotage your sex drive.

You know how it's easy for you to have an erection in the middle of the night when you're by yourself, or when you're alone watching a porno? That's because you're not worrying about anything and are in a mental state where you've let go of any pressure about performing.

So when you simply let yourself go and stop thinking about specific outcomes like "I must get hard," then things work out fine for you.

In fact, don't even think about this concept called "sex" when you're going all the way with a woman. Just focus on the moment.

Think about only your penis, and how good it feels to put it inside her throbbing, slippery vagina. Who cares if she comes? All that matters is that you're feeling good, and that when you have your release of sperm inside her, you'll feel deeply relaxed and content.

You say you're a "two pump chump" (an

affliction that one-third of men have by the way)? Who cares! The reason you came so fast is that the sex felt so good! (Besides, we'll cover how to last longer in a later chapter, but only consult it if you don't have any problems with self-esteem-based sexual anxiety.)

If you're not in a monogamous relationship, then another way to eliminate your sexual anxiety is to have no-strings attached one night stands. This frees you to not care one bit about how the chick thinks, since you won't see her again once you two go your separate ways in the morning.

Remember that all of this telling yourself things like "who cares what she thinks" is a mental exercise to reduce your anxiety. It's not me advocating that you turn into a jerk or anything.

But there's also another quick and easy way to eliminate your anxiety, which is the exact opposite of this advice.

This quick and easy way is a tried and true one mentioned in the Kama Sutra, a sex manual from ancient India, which is still consulted frequently to this day because of its exotic pearls of sexual wisdom and secrets.

What you do is forget about yourself and turn off all self-analyzing, self-thoughts, and self-focusing. In fact, **pretend that you don't even exist.**

Instead, focus on her. Pretend you *are* her. Imagine her feelings and the pleasure she is having. Visualize your sexual encounter from her point of view.

I would suggest avoiding aphrodisiac drugs, since you don't need them (because your mind is the most powerful aphrodisiac, and you can change your thought patterns without use of drugs). The evidence of most aphrodisiac drugs such as ginseng is shaky at best.

However, there have been some promising animal studies on yohimbe, which is derived from the bark of an African tree. If you want to go that route, Drugstore.com usually has some good deals.

A lot of people suggest alcohol. While alcohol doesn't do anything for you sexually such as increase blood flow to your penis (the way Yohimbe is reputed to), and in fact depresses your sexual function, moderate consumption of alcohol does provide temporary stress relief by lowering your inhibitions.

If you do decide to drink, I recommend you use wine instead of beer, since the latter can foul the taste of your semen.

The key point about your mind is that all your thoughts and your memories are under your control. If you tell yourself things like, "I must perform well" and "I've got to get it up," you're setting yourself up for failure and depression.

On the other hand, if you program your mind with things like, "I don't give a fuck what she thinks" and "this feels really good when I put my dick inside her," then you will be focusing only on the here and now, and you will overcome any sort of anxiety you have about sex.

Remember, as the man, you're giving the woman pleasure merely by cuddling with her in bed. Her alternative is wrapping her legs around a pillow, by herself in bed. So you're doing her a great favor. So stop worrying and start enjoying yourself in bed!

How to Be Her Best Lover Ever by John Alexander
(c) Copyright 2005, John Alexander Enterprises, Inc.

How to Give Your Woman a Hand Job

A woman's clit is somewhat comparable to your penis. Basically, it's like a little penis buried under a ton of foreskin.

The first rule of touching your woman's pussy is to make sure your finger is wet. The clit is delicate and very sensitive, especially at first.

Like so many other parts of your sexual arsenal, your mindset is everything. Keep this in mind:

You are touching her to please yourself, not her.

This is totally counter-intuitive and you may initially disagree with it, but hear me out.

When you take the mindset that you're caressing your woman's pussy in order to please yourself, it takes all the pressure off of you.

With the pressure taken off of you, you'll be able to relax and not go too fast or firm with your fingers.

And guess what? Being focused only on your own pleasure also takes the pressure off of her. If a woman knows that you're enjoying yourself, she has no tension about trying to stoke your ego by making you think she's enjoying it more than she is.

Focus on her vulva when you're caressing it. As you focus on it, stroke it and massage it slowly.

Keep your finger wet by putting it into her vagina. Then pull your wet finger out and stroke her clit and vulva.

Enjoy the awesome sensations you feel from touching her in her most private area.

Remember to always keep thinking about her pussy as you're massaging it. If your mind wanders, bring it back to the task at hand. Think about how good she feels on your fingertips.

This is another reason why it's important to move slowly. If you move fast and become outcome oriented (i.e., trying to make her feel good), you'll get bored.

Also, slowness with your handjob is important for her sensory pleasure. I can't emphasize this enough. Guys want to go fast and forcefully and get the job done, like when you were an inexperienced teenager jacking off as quick as you could.

Unless your woman is getting close to orgasm, keep your finger pressure soft and slow.

Also, be sure to always keep both hands busy. While one hand strokes her hungry clit, have the other playing with her nipples, anus, perineum, hair, etc.

Guide to Giving Oral

Of all the skills you can have in bed, cunnilingus is the most important. Being good at eating pussy is the ultimate attribute of a great lover.

When a woman has found a man who is good at eating pussy, she's found something more addictive than the most powerful drugs, and as long as he isn't an ax murderer or something, she won't even think about letting go of him.

Just imagine... you'll have the power to bring your woman to orgasm with your mouth and tongue, and she will want you as never before. She won't even think about going out with other guys, because she'll know that no one can please her the way you can.

Most men do an adequate job with thrusting their penises in and out of a woman's vagina, but they are unskilled when it comes to cunnilingus. So getting good at this is a "low hanging fruit" towards becoming the best lover your woman's ever had.

Don't expect good feedback from your woman, either. Most women will tell you everything's great, in order to not damage the notoriously fragile male ego. The only way you can really gauge how well you're doing with oral sex--and sex in general--is whether or not she orgasms.

But the ironic thing is that you can't think about whether your woman orgasms, because if you have that as your goal, you will put too much pressure on the situation and it will fail.

When you start out, surely you'll have adopted the "go slow" strategy and ingrained it as part of your bedroom personality by now (if not, consult the chapter of the guide that discusses why slowness is important.)

In general, you'll want to gradually work your way up to eating her pussy, and then when you're eating it, work your way gradually towards her clit, and then gradually working up the intensity of your clitoral licking.

The secret to good oral sex on a woman is to have her know that...

You Enjoy Eating Her Pussy.

The reason is that despite the efforts of campaigns such as The Vagina Monologues, a lot of women still view their pussies as something "down there" that's "dirty" and unappealing.

Additionally, a lot of men too do not enjoy eating pussy, which doesn't help matters. By the way, simply enjoying cunnilingus separates you above a lot of men.

How to Enjoy Eating Pussy

You say you don't enjoy eating pussy? It's time to change that. In fact, in order to become her best lover ever, you must force yourself to change your opinion.

This is entirely possible, because studies have shown that repeated exposure to tastes makes us accustomed to the taste, which then improves our opinion of that taste.

Few coffee drinkers, beer drinkers, and smokers liked the taste of those products the first time they consumed them. Yet with time, they grew to enjoy the tastes.

Neurologists call this phenomenon the "mere exposure effect."

The more we expose ourselves to a particular stimulus (no matter what it is), the more we like it. Brain scans would show that the more we taste a woman's clit and mound and the juices that come out of her pussy, the more chemicals such as dopamine flood our brains, indicating that we have more positive emotions tied to the taste, smell, feel, and sight of pussy.

The bottom line:

Secret #1: The More You Eat Pussy, The Better You Will Like It.

So even if you don't like it at first, just keep plowing through, because eventually you will.

But suppose you don't have any pussies around that you can eat. Instead what you can do is expose yourself to similar flavors (which I will explain in a second). That way when you do go down on a woman, you will savor every moment of it.

A healthy (non-yeast infected) vagina contains a bacteria called *Lactobacillus acidophilus*. This is the same bacteria found in plain yogurt and in a dairy drink called kefir (which you can find at your local health food store).

In fact, although no two women taste the same (and the same woman can vary in taste depending on her diet and where she is in her monthly hormone cycle), as a general rule I've found that the taste of a woman's pussy most closely approximates that of plain yogurt. So learn to like that food!

While semen has a high pH level, the vagina is acidic (with a pH between 3.8 and 4.5). The following are foods and beverages with the same pH range as the average vagina. To accustom yourself better to the acidic taste of a woman, consume more of the following:
- Apples.
- Apricots.
- Blackberries.
- Cream Cheese (good when spread on celery and broccoli, two sperm-friendly

foods).
- Cherries.
- Ketchup.
- Kumquats.
- Mangoes.
- Nectarines.
- Oranges.
- Orange Juice.
- Peaches.
- Pears.
- Plums.
- Prunes.
- Prune Juice.
- Raisins.
- Sweet tangerines.
- Tomatoes.
- Tomato Juice.
- Tomato Paste.
- V8 Vegetable Juice.

If you've never tasted a woman before, a vagina can be either a little bit sweet or a little salty, sometimes with a musky smell and taste if she's not yet gushing wet. And when it's around the time of her period, there's a bit of an iron smell and strong musk taste.

For a lighter and sweeter-tasting vagina, encourage your woman to eat healthier and avoid junk food, strong flavors (especially garlic and onions), excessive red meat, and cigarettes.

Learning to Love The Vagina

Not only does it taste good, but enjoy the beauty of the pussy as well. The bush in front. In the places where she shaves, she has that tiny peach fuzz which glistens when she's wet. Her vaginal lips become bright red when she's hungry to have your hard dick inside her.

There is nothing in this world prettier than the center of a woman's femininity... the love hole that brings you so much pleasure.

The vagina is the center of a woman's being. It is what makes her feminine. For me, it is the center of the universe. Meditate on the vagina. Fall in love with it. It is the source of the greatest pleasure and happiness you can ever find.

And for your woman, the vagina brings her such unbounded joy. There's nothing more spectacular than having your dick inside a woman as she shudders under an uncontrollable orgasm, as you feel her throbbing contractions on your manhood.

Even the most drop-dead gorgeous women can be--as mentioned previously--timid about their vaginas, due to societal conditioning and possibly former boyfriends who insulted them when they were at their most vulnerable. As a result, you need to make your woman aware in no uncertain terms how appealing and desirable you find her body.

Not only should you qualify her by telling her how beautiful you find her pussy, but you should also communicate it through her reactions. Let your jaw drop and say, "Wow!" when you get her panties off. When going down on her, sniff in her scent deeply and say, "Ahh you smell so sweet, baby!" Lick her and moan, "Mmmmmmm!"

By the way, being responsive and communicative is another secret to success. It separates you from almost all other guys.

While women usually are loud in bed, men are often silent, except for a slight moan when they come. Forget being the "strong silent type" in bed.

Secret #2:
Express your excitement freely...
and she will in turn be more excited.

I have had a lot of women tell me how much they love the fact that I'm loud.

Your Eating Style

Every woman is unique when it comes to what she enjoys when you're eating her pussy. My current woman, after being in a relationship with me for a year, is usually so aroused to begin with when we have sex that she practically shoves my head directly onto her clit and wants me to lick hard.

But you'll want to experiment and always try new things, yet go slower than you think you should. Watch her reactions and listen to her moans. You'll quickly discover where she likes to be licked and how hard she wants you to build up to.

As a general rule, approach her clitoris slowly and teasingly. Remember, you're heating her up gradually. This will intensify her ecstasy.

Of course, when you're having sex, you shouldn't go directly into cunnilingus. First go through the various stages of escalation--i.e., French kissing her, passionately stroking her hot body all over, and sucking her tits.

So when do you decide that it's time to go down on her? As a basic rule, you should do it when she becomes soaking wet down there. Test it by touching her pussy with your finger. (Don't make it obvious to her that you're doing that, however.) If she is thoroughly gushing with her womanly juices, then you will soon be ready to dive into her honey pot.

Pussy eating comes late in the sexual intercourse game. Well before your mouth is ready to consume her clit, you should have gone through the phases of touching, kissing, and tasting her everywhere else.

Once you reach the cunnilingal phase, start by enjoying her breasts and nipples one last time. Perhaps you can coat her nipples with the love juices you collected from her pussy lips, and then lick the delicious nectar from her nipple.

Kiss downward from there towards the center of her womanhood, concentrating on your own sense of smell, taking in her bodily aromas. As you do this, you'll notice that as you get closer and closer to the area normally covered by panties, the more you can smell the wonderful scent of a horny woman.

Here you should feel free to say "mmmm" as you breathe in the pleasant scent of her wetness. If you want, add something like, "Baby, I love the way your juices smell!" For a woman to get maximum enjoyment from having her pussy eaten, she needs to know that you enjoy it.

Continue going down below her belly button toward her bush, but lift your head so that your lips are no longer touching her. Pause right above her crotch, sniffing in her womanly goodness.

Move downward still and start kissing the inner parts of her thighs, first one, going upward towards her pussy (coming close but pulling away at the last minute). Then move to her other thigh and do something similar. Brush your lips and tongue along her thighs ever so slightly. Move lazily.

Come perilously close to her vulva and clit, and then pull away. Enjoy the way she's feeling more and more teased into a new height of horniness.

Kiss a bit more around her inner thighs, and then move in. There are creases on either side of the vulva, where the legs meet the cunt. Lick there. Inhale her scent deeply, since you've reached her dripping pussy!

Rub your face on her bush or (if she's shaved bare) the area where her bush would be. With your hands, lightly massage her cunt.

Then brush your lips and nose lightly like a feather over her wet slit. Do it with such a soft touch that it makes her even wetter, with an increasing amount of anticipation.

While you're working with your mouth, keep going back to caressing her intimately with your hands, massaging her breasts and inner thighs.

At this point, she should be practically begging you for more. Watch her behavior. Is she nudging her pelvis closer to you? Then that means it's time for you to put your lips directly on her slit.

Kiss her vulva slowly and lightly at first, and then with more pressure. Stick your tongue out and move it side to side to open up her lips.

During this time, gently spread her legs with your hands. Not only does this open her vaginal lips up for your tongue, but this establishes you as the alpha male in total control of her pleasure, which makes her even more wet.

As the man going down on his woman, you are in charge of her pleasure. She is at your tender mercy.

Make sure you're in a comfortable position, because you're going to be down there awhile! Be relaxed. You don't want your muscles to be stiff. And the whole time you're going down on your woman, hold her and constantly kiss her. You are giving her a great gift of love.

Using your fingers, lightly pull her outer lips apart to enjoy her inner lips. Sniff them deeply, taking in the scent, and lightly lick them the way you licked soft ice cream as a kid. (See, all that junk food you ate in your youth did come in handy some day!) Gently blow your hot breath on her and then lap up the juices around her pussy lips.

Having spread her legs and opened up her lips, you can now slowly work your tongue into her vagina. Stick your tongue in all the way. Imagine your tongue is a penis and fuck her with it.

Suck her juices into your mouth, savor the taste, and swallow. Swirl your tongue into her love tunnel. Enjoy how smooth, hot, and sticky it is.

This teases your woman even further because, while she loves having your tongue in her vagina, there's another place where she wants it even more--her clitoris!

So at this point, move your tongue out of her vagina, enjoying her wonderful womanly tastes as you do. Again, don't be mum about how much you enjoy it.

A lot of men are dead silent when eating pussy, which can confuse and stress out women... this is because she'll want to know what you're thinking. Are you still enjoying being down there? Are you getting impatient because your tongue's getting tired and you wish she'd hurry up and come?

Often, a woman's thoughts sabotage her sexual pleasure. You can interrupt her negative thought patterns by saying, "Mmmmm your pussy's so goood!"

You want her to understand that you're eating her pussy not because you're sacrificing yourself to make her feel good, but that you simply enjoy doing it. Because she knows that you enjoy it, this gives her permission to relax and enjoy herself. " After all," she thinks, "I'm making my man feel good when he eats my pussy!"

Lick and suck on her inner lips, tugging on them softly. Use the same pressure on those lips that you would on the lips she has on her face. (In fact, one technique that helps you to be a good lover is to imagine that you're licking, kissing, and nibbling on her regular lips... and then use that same pressure on her pussy lips.)

Touch your tongue to her perineum. At this point, you could do even a bit of analingus if you wish. (Flicking your tongue on your woman's anus is completely optional and not necessary for a woman's sexual pleasure.)

Move back up from her perineum, licking her groove and sucking on her lips.

Work your tongue slowly up to the top of her slit, where her clitoral hood is. Start licking it.

Now that you're licking her sweet spot, the center of her ecstasy--an area with a concentration of nerves that's much higher than the penis--you can gradually move up to being more and more direct and forceful.

Swirl your tongue around at first. One tip that works for a girl who you haven't got a lot of experience with is to lick the letters of the alphabet--A, B, C, D, etc.--on her clit.

Licking the alphabet was a tip that I got from comedian Sam Kinnison back in the day. I like it because it's a good crutch to keep teasing a woman into ever-deepening sexual frenzy. It keeps you going slow, yet in (to her) patterns that change randomly into various swirls and up-and-down motions.

That way, from her perspective, you keep it interesting as her arousal increases, rather than having your motions become redundant.

Licking the alphabet is also a way to pass the time. Eating pussy in many ways is a game of letting the clock run out. The average woman takes 5 to 20 minutes of clitoral stimulation before she orgasms, so you need to keep your mind occupied in order to not become impatient.

Sometimes I like to even write words or sentences with my tongue. (For the space between words, I flick my tongue into her vaginal opening.)

By the way, try to not put much stress on yourself about whether your woman comes or not. Unlike with us men, it's not always necessary for a woman to achieve orgasm for her to be sexually satisfied. So it might be that you'll quit cunnilingus after awhile, without her coming, in order to put your dick in.

How to tell you're doing a good job – watch for her legs to shutter as she moves into deeper pleasure.

Because the clitoris is so sensitive to touch, you need to keep getting her more and more aroused before you can increase the direct pressure on it.

Once she's extremely highly aroused, get her clitoral hood out of the way. This can be accomplished a number of ways. One is to coat your two index fingers with her juices and then gently pull back the hood to lick the clit directly.

Another way is to push upward on her clit using your lower lip and jaw. While you've pushed her clit up, lick the portion that juts out.

A third way is to put your thumbs just above her pubic bone area and then push upward on her lower abdomen, exposing more of her clit and vagina.

Pull her clitoral hood up with your upper lip and her vulva lips apart with your bottom lip. Then lick hard against her clitoris, which by this point has become engorged and pushed out through the clitoral hood. Flick your tongue quickly.

The Suction Technique

When she's as massively aroused as she can be, suck her clit into your mouth. This stimulates it to become even further engorged with blood, intensifying her pleasure.

Keep sucking harder and harder, as hard as she can take.

When pulling her clit into your mouth, you create suction. Then you can let go and her clit will pop out of your mouth.

Repeat the process, sucking her clit into her mouth and then letting it pop back out.

This drives her wild.

How to Move Her Towards a Mind-Blowing Orgasm

Imagine your tongue is no longer a tongue. Imagine it's turned into your index finger, so that way you'll press more firmly with it than you normally would with your tongue.

As a woman's pleasure increases, often she'll feel like she wants something inside her.

So, put your pointer finger inside her. It rockets a woman's pleasure to the moon when you finger bang her at the same time your tongue is enjoying her clit.

But don't do this by simply poking your finger in and out the way they do it in porn movies. Instead stroke her, which you'll find on her front wall, about one inch above her vaginal opening.

Start to finger bang her as her clitoral stimulation increases. Read the section on G-Spot stimulation for more details, but basically you should start out soft with her G-Spot, moving your finger all around as you're eating her pussy, and then become firmer and focus directly on the squishy tissue of her G-Spot. Don't just jam your fingers into her vagina.

Tip: Always make sure your fingernails are

clipped short and smooth. If you slice her from the inside with a sharp fingernail, she will become sore, and the last thing you want is for your woman to associate soreness with your touch.

Another top: This thing you're putting in her not only has a fingernail, but it's also made of bone... which makes it much harder than a penis. So be gentle.

A lot of men recommend putting a second finger into her vagina, but I believe that is a mistake. Why? Because, although she would indeed get added pleasure from a second finger...

You don't want anything competing with your penis.

The typical guy's dick is about the width of two of fingers, give or take a few millimeters. As a guy, it's better for you if by far the most exquisite, filled-up-vagina feeling a woman gets is from your penis, and your penis only.

Experiment with different ways of licking her clit, since every woman is unique. How fast should you go? Watch her breathing to quicken. Watch her nipples to stiffen. Watch her skin to flush red. Watch her muscles begin to tremble.

Watch her signals to see what she responds to the most. Once you've found a way that she indicates gives her the maximum amount of pleasure, keep doing it that way! Now is not the time to change what you do. Keep at it until she orgasms.

A lot of men make a mistake when they hear her moan loudly and realize they've hit a sweet spot on her clit. The mistake they make is to think that they should go harder and faster. Often this is a mistake.

Ever notice how a woman will scream "Don't stop!"? That doesn't mean "Put on more pressure."

The bottom line: if she tenses her muscles and moans extra loudly because you've hit a sweet spot, keep going at exactly the same speed and intensity and it will drive her towards orgasm.

She'll move her pelvis up and down as the pleasure keeps increasing. When she does this, move with her. Keep her clit in your mouth.

Don't stop eating her pussy at this point! She's drawing closer to orgasm, so keep it up.

As she starts to have her orgasm, keep stimulating her clit.

As she comes down from the peak of her orgasm, slow down your G spot stroking and clit licking.

A woman in orgasm is a beauty to behold.

How to Be Her Best Lover Ever by John Alexander
(c) Copyright 2005, John Alexander Enterprises, Inc.

But how do you tell when she's for real and when she's faking it? Well, you can look for certain involuntary bodily responses on her part.

This is similar to when you were in elementary school and your teachers and school counselors could easily tell when you were lying... with the way you had extra long pauses in your sentences, as you struggled to keep your story consistent.

Look for several indicators of orgasm:
- Her vaginal muscles pulse.
- Her vagina releases more fluid.
- Her toes curl.
- She breathes heavily.
- She contracts her muscles, often by grabbing something (like your back) and squeezing.
- She moans towards the end of the orgasm.

Once a woman orgasms, she temporarily feels very sensitive at her clit. Move down to her lips and lick them softly, tasting her sweet juices.

The best time to fuck a girl is right after she's come, because her vaginal walls are pulsing and contracting, and one of the best feelings for her is to have her vagina contracting around a rock solid dick.

Kiss her up from her hold, passing over clit, kissing her mound, then her belly, then her two tits, then her upper chest, then her neck, and then pass over her face toward her forehead.

Make sure you've swallowed any vaginal juices in your mouth and licked any juices off your lips. You know how you don't relish the thought of French kissing a woman who has your come in her mouth? Assume it's the same thing for her.

Once you're sure you've swallowed any of her vaginal juices still in and around your mouth, softly kiss her on her lips. put your arms under her back and shoulders and hold her tight.

This is a point where a woman feels extremely close to you, so blow into her ear and (if you're at the proper point in your relationship) tell her you love her.

Once a woman has orgasmed from you having eaten her pussy, she'll be having aftershocks in which her vaginal walls keep contracting. So that means it's the perfect time for you to put your penis inside her.

Advanced Tips For Eating Pussy

Listen to her moans. Whenever you hear a moan when you do a particular tongue motion on her vulva, clit, or vagina, remember it. Go back to that motion and keep doing it for a couple minutes.

Be consistent in your motions when tonguing her. While it's good to shift around what you do, shift gradually.

Women often don't want to tell their men that they're doing anything other than a perfect job at cunnilingus. So if you hear from her that you're a stallion with your tongue, but you're still not totally sure about how much pressure to use with your tongue and mouth on her vaginal lips and clit, try the following trick:

Lie on your back and have your woman sit on your face.

Not only does that give you a close up view of your woman's exquisite body, but it puts her in control of how much stimulation she gets. Too hard, and she'll move up or to the side so that she gets more indirect pleasure on her clit. Lick her too soft, and she'll grind harder against your mouth and face.

This also puts her in control of how long the cunnilingus will last. She may stay on you even after she comes, in order to grind for orgasm #2. Or she may be having trouble coming and simply want your penis inside her, at which point she slips off of your face and sits on your penis.

Watch and learn from amateur lesbian porn. Nobody knows how to eat pussy like a woman... notice how soft women go on each other (and then harder when the time is right)? Next time you eat pussy, imagine you're a lesbian trapped in a man's body.

What to do when her clit is hyper-sensitive. Unfortunately, some women always find direct clitoral stimulation to be too intense for them, no matter how aroused they get. I've found two solutions to this:
1. Lick to the *side* of (not above or below) their clit. This takes a long time, but it will get them to orgasm.
2. Lick their clit while their panties are still on. (Use a steady, regular up and down motion with your tongue.) This gets them to orgasm faster than number 1, but of course you lose the advantage of having your tongue directly on her luscious lower lips.

Whenever you're doing cunnilingus on a chick, use your hands throughout the process, in the dominant manner of an alpha male. This turns almost all women into maniacs who worship you! While eating her pussy, you can for example:
- Hold her hands, intertwining your fingers into hers.
- Massage her breasts.
- Grab her hot ass, caressing her soft cheeks, teasing the area around her anus (and perhaps even ease a finger into it if the two of you have crossed that barrier), and then move your hands down to her hips.

About teasing that anus of hers during cunnilingus. Here's how to do it...

First, like the outer lips of the vagina, the anus requires that you finger be pre-moistened as well. Use her vagina juices to wet your finger.

The best strategy for anal stimulation is to concentrate on rubbing her vaginal juices into the skin around her anus.

Put your fingertip in slightly if you want. Tease her there are go slow. Again, don't just jam it in all the way to the hilt, or else the jolt of pain she feels from it may shock her out of her sexual arousal.

Also, remember that the finger stimulation that you're doing is always secondary to the cunnilingus.

The main stimulation you're giving her is on her clit... so anything else is just a supplement to boost her more closer to edge of the "Big O"... and then when she does have it, the added stimulation of your finger on her anus will make her orgasm even more powerful.

She may even scream uncontrollably during it.

After finishing fingering her anus, don't put that same finger into her vagina. The anus contains bacteria that if introduced into her vagina can cause her to develop a yeast infection.

Tongue Exercises

Did you know you can increase your tongue's strength and endurance by 200% or more?

The four exercises below have been contributed by Matthew Doening, author of The Ugly Man's Guide to Picking Up Beautiful Women, which you can visit through a special link I set up for him at: www.herbestlover.com/uglyman

Exercise 1:

Stick your tongue as far out of your mouth as possible, and try to touch your nose. Once in this position, hold the same muscle groups still and begin moving your tongue around. Practice in sets, moving the tongue clockwise, counterclockwise, and up and down.

Exercise 2:

With a loose jaw, point your tongue while simultaneously trying to keep your tongue in constant contact with the the top and bottom of your mouth.

Once you are in this position, practice moving your tongue in and out of your mouth.

For the more advanced student, try keeping

your mouth closed and circling your tongue around inside of it, while of course, maintaining position. An extension to the advanced exercise is trying to dissolve a lifesaver held in your teeth from the inside out.

Exercise 3:

Stick your tongue straight out of your mouth, trying to keep your tongue flat and relaxed. While holding this position, practice slowly curling the wide tip of the tongue upward, downward and side-to-side. Practice in five sets of ten, holding each move for 2 seconds.

Exercise 4:

Keep your tongue relaxed and open your mouth. Move your tongue in and out of your mouth forwards and in both directions. Practice in five sets of twenty.

But you'll want to experiment and always try new things, yet go slower than you think you should. Watch her reactions and listen to her moans. You'll quickly discover where she likes to be licked and how hard she wants you to build up to.

John Alexander's Final Thoughts About Cunnilingus

In general, I have found it's best if I have a

woman give me oral sex first when I have a choice in the matter. (If the woman is not sufficiently excited about having sex, then you should perform oral on her to get her into the mood.)

The reason to have her go first is that the male refractory period lasts 5 to 60 minutes under even the most intense stimulation. So when you think about it, what qualifies as...

> a) something to keep her occupied for 5 to 60 minutes (depending on how fast or slow you go)?

and...

> b) the most intense sexual stimulation for yourself to get yourself back in the mood (because let's face it... there's nothing more stimulating than a close-up view of a naked woman)?

You got it – performing oral sex on her.

Probably the best part about going down on a woman, aside from how much you enjoy the sensations it brings you, is that it allows you to achieve the highest form of pleasure: the joy of knowing you've made your woman feel so good.

Her G-Spot

With your woman lying on her back, put your pointer finger inside her, curling the finger up a bit, like you would if you were motioning a person to "come here."

To find her G-spot, feel around the inside of her vagina with your pointer finger. Notice how smooth her vagina is, search for a tiny squishy spot (a shallow mound), not smooth like the rest of her love tunnel, that's behind where you think her bladder is. That's the G-spot.

The G-Spot is the woman's equivalent of your prostate gland. It produces sex hormones for her and has a high concentration of nerve endings.

Press on it steadily in an upward motion and she will have more and more stimulation building. To rocket a woman towards orgasm, combine cunnilingus with this G-spot stimulation.

The first time you ever stimulate your woman's G-spot, she may complain that she needs to pee. Tell her that the feeling will pass and that she should allow herself to relax and absorb the sensations you're giving her.

As the feeling does pass, she will become massively lubed in her vagina, and if she comes, vaginal fluid will come gushing out.

An orgasm that comes from having her G-Spot combined with eating her clit has a different feeling to a woman that clitoral stimulation by itself. The former type of orgasm causes her to gush out fluid and feels kind of like an "explosion" to women, from what I've been told. A clitoris-only orgasm, by contrast, feels like an implosion.

It's an amazing feeling for you at that point if you insert your penis, because of the massive amount of lubrication and her throbbing inner pussy walls.

When you press on her G-Spot, use gentle pressure, and go slow with your rhythm rather than fast. Basically G-Spot stimulation is a supplement to the main clitoral stimulation that you're doing with your mouth, so there's no reason to shift your main focus from her clit to her G-Spot.

As I said, the primary movement you should use will be the "come here" gesture with your pointer finger. There are other ways to finger her G-Spot as well:
- Circling the G-Spot with your finger. When done at the right strategic moment - let's say you suddenly switch to this after several minutes of the "come here" motion - this can be a surprise weapon in your arsenal way to push a woman over the top.
- Switching hands. Let's face it, your

finger can get tired! However, with enough practice, you can build up your muscular stamina. The pointer finger of my right hand can last about 10 minutes before it needs a rest, and my left pointer finger lasts about half that.

How to Insert Your Penis

As far as the entire process of sexual intercourse is concerned, this is actually the easiest thing to do. If you've done everything else correctly up to that point, she'll be massively aroused and practically begging you to "fuck me hard!"

So you just put in your penis and thrust into your woman like an animal!

With that said, however, pay close attention to your woman's non-verbal signals to you...
- Watch how she moves her pelvis. Women tend to move their pelvises without really thinking about it, so chances are slim and none that she'll fake pelvic motions.
- If she thrusts her pelvis toward you and/or puts her hands on your ass and pulls you toward her, it means she wants you to thrust in your penis with more pressure and put it in deeply.
- If she moves her pelvis away from you and/or puts her hands on your chest in a blocking gesture, it means you could be hitting her uterus (which can be painful for a woman) and should go shallower.
- Watch whether her skin flushes red and watch her breathing... panting

and breathing harder means her pleasure is rising.
- Listen to her moaning.

There are certain angles from which you can thrust in your penis and have her feel even more delight. For example, if your penis scrapes against her G-Spot, it could send her into dizzying heights.

So watch for her obvious signals (many of which are hard for a woman to fake) and you can read her desires with no mystery.

But mostly don't worry about it. The best thing you can do during sex is to lose yourself completely in lust and not even think about whether you're doing it "right."

Sexual Positions

You may have your standard position that brings you the most pleasure. That's okay, but for a woman, variety is important.

There's little to be gained from imitating porn videos where they have 6 positions in 6 minutes, but as a general rule try to change your sexual position about 10% to 20% of the time.

And when you do try out a new position, you have the most successful lovemaking session by doing one of two things:
1. Sticking with that new position until you and/or she have an orgasm.
2. Sticking with that new position for awhile, but then switching back to your standard position when you're ready to drive toward orgasm.

It's good to give your woman a variety of positions because it allows you to hit her vagina from different angles, causing her to have totally new sensations (all caused by you, big guy!)

It's also good for you because making love to your woman lets you view her gorgeous body from different perspectives. And it gives you whole new sensations.

How to Be Her Best Lover Ever by John Alexander
(c) Copyright 2005, John Alexander Enterprises, Inc.

Of course, there are literally hundreds of sexual positions. (And there are even whole websites devoted to the topic.)

Most of the positions are only good for contortionists, however. The following positions are not only realistic, but they also cover all the bases when it comes to feeling all the sensations possible for you and her.

The Missionary Position

The two of you are lying down, with you on top.

Women perceive this as being the "safe" position, so it makes them feel the most comfortable and closest to you. So use this especially when you're with a woman who's sexually inexperienced (e.g., a college girl).

The missionary position is also the most intimate. The two of you merge together in body and soul when you make love to her missionary-style.

There are several variations of the missionary position, and you should experiment to find them. Here are a few:

Totally Tantric

Lie flat on top of her, with every part of your body touching every part of hers. Keep your legs straight behind you and close together.

Resting some of your weight on your elbows, use your arms to pull yourself in and out of her.

Caressing Her From the Inside

She spreads her legs wide. You get on top of her, with your legs spread.

Have most of your weight resting on your legs. Thrust your penis in and out of her by using your legs to rock your pelvis.

By the way, this variation of the missionary position is easier than it sounds. In fact, it will be a lot more pleasurable if you keep your muscles relaxed rather than tense.

The Red-Hot Thrusting Trick

Grab her ass with both of your hands and pull her towards you for each thrust.

A Tighter Grip on You

Rather than have her spread her legs or wrap them around you the way your woman normally will in the missionary position, have her keep them close together while you penetrate her.

This will cause an ultra-tight grip on you, so use with caution!

Doggie Style

There are several advantages to this position, which by the way should only be done with your woman if she feels sexually comfortable with you and is sexually experienced with you.

- You'll like that you can gyrate harder by pulling her hips, causing you to feel more sensations on your penis.
- Her breasts hang freely and are just dying for your touch.
- It's a nice view of her ass!
- You can finger her anus if the two of you are into that sort of thing.
- Psychologically, women consider this to be a "fuck me like an animal" position.

Girl on Top

She rides you like a cowgirl. This is, by the way, an excellent gauge as to whether your woman is too heavy... if she can no longer painlessly be on top, it's time for her to diet (or for you to start looking elsewhere for love).

There are three huge advantages to this position:
1. She does all the work. You can relax and be lazy.
2. It's like watching a porno--with you in it!
3. Your hands can explore all over her body.

The Pelvis Slam

With your woman lying on her back, put her legs over your shoulders. This causes your pelvis and hers to grind together.

Her legs are in such a position that her vagina will feel tighter, plus she'll get the sensations of your penis coming in from a different angle.

The Ultimate Front-Row View

The woman lies on the bed, on her back, with her ass hanging over the edge. You, standing on the floor, hold her legs in your arms.

Then rock back and forth.

This is the best view, and from the best angle, you can have of a woman's body.

In From the Side

Have the woman lie on her back, while you lie on your side, with your body in roughly a 90 degree angle in relation to hers.

Lift her leg up, and then enter her.

Advantages to this position:
- You get to feel the side of her vagina on your penis.
- She gets unusual sensations she doesn't

get from other positions.
- You get a good view of your penis moving in and out of her vagina.

How to Give Her the Orgasm To End All Orgasms

You won't read this sex technique anywhere else. It's a John Alexander patented move. I'm sharing it right here for the first time.

Did you know that right after - that is, *within one second* following- a woman's orgasm, she's got the capability to blow her fuses?

If you time this technique correctly, you can have your woman melt right in front of you, fill the house with her screams, and have her babbling like she's drunk.

Most girls are afraid of behaving this way in front of their men because they don't want to lose all control of themselves and shriek like a madwoman in front of you.

And almost no guys will ever figure out this technique because it has you do the opposite of what your instincts tell you to.

So here's what you do. Right at the moment a girl's at the peak of her orgasm through oral sex, and as she's beginning to come down from her orgasm, her clit becomes sensitive and she'll want you to slow down.

Probably she'll nudge your head away with her fingers or push you away by your shoulders. She may even say something like, "Hold on for a second while I catch my breath."

So right at moment, don't back off. Instead take charge. And do it with lightning speed. Force her legs wide open, hold down her hands, and fuck her as hard and fast as you can.

She will resist... but you must persist past that resistance.

After only a half dozen pumps (about four or five seconds), she will have the greatest orgasm of her entire life. So much vaginal fluid will gush out of her that your sheets will be soaked.

After such a tremendous orgasm, your woman will feel very delicate and have rapid mood swings. She could be giggly one second and burst into tears the next.

It's *crucial* at this moment to cuddle with her. Cuddle for a long time, because she won't come back into reality for a long time.

She's exposed a big vulnerability to you by losing all emotional control, so it's vital that you tell her everything's fine and you love that she came so hard.

And by the way, you've now got a woman who's devoted to you for rest of her life!

How to Be Her Best Lover Ever by John Alexander
(c) Copyright 2005, John Alexander Enterprises, Inc.

How to Reduce Your Refractory Period to be the Best Lover She's Ever Had... or Ever Will Have!

A lot of men wonder how they can last longer. They come up with strategies for it. Maybe they'll think of baseball stats while making love. Or they'll think of what they did that day at work.

What a terrible thing to occupy your mind during sex! This interferes with your full enjoyment of it.

I mean, it's cool to delay your own orgasms because that means your woman gets more pleasure, but why not get the maximum enjoyment yourself out of the sexual intercourse? Rather than fighting off your ejaculations...

Wouldn't it be better if you could come over and over again?

Trust me, the second time you make love, right after you've ejaculated the first time, you'll last a lot longer, without you having to even give it a second thought.

There's no point in denying yourself the full pleasure of sex or trying to blunt the nice sensations your body feels. Instead embrace the pleasure! This chapter will teach you how.

Ready for the most amazing part? You can become multi-orgasmic through basic muscle exercises, taking only a matter of minutes each time you do them.

Okay, so here's the deal. You have a muscle that controls your penis. Every time you come, this muscle contracts and shoots out the semen.

If you want to be able to ejaculate more powerfully, and more often... in fact so often that you have true multiple orgasm ability, then build up this muscle.

This little-known body part is called the pubococcugeus or PC muscle for short. You can tell which muscle I'm talking about in two ways. It's the muscle that contracts:
- When you ejaculate.
- When you're urinating and you want to stop the flow of urine mid-stream.
- When you have an erection and want to make your penis move up and down.

You can find your PC muscle by putting your finger behind your scrotum. Then do one of the above three things - either simulate that you are coming (or make yourself come for real), go take a piss and then stop yourself from peeing, or get an erection and make your penis move. You'll feel your PC muscle contract at that point.

For almost all men, the PC muscle is vastly underdeveloped. The good news is that you'll notice rapid, dramatic increases in your PC muscle strength.

So it's time to get started. Here's how to do it...

Contract your PC muscle and hold it for as long as you can, until your PC muscle literally is not able to stay contracted any longer. Rest for a minute, and then do it again. Do this every three days.

Make sure that your ass and ab muscles don't contract. It's common when you're new to doing PC contractions, and your muscles are weak, to want to move other muscles. Don't.

What you want to do is feel relaxed when you work your PC muscle. Don't try to get an erection or anything like that, because you can work your PC muscle when your penis is flaccid.

The best place to do PC exercises, I've found, is in the car. You're sitting a relaxed position anyway, and usually you've got nothing better to do but to contract your PC.

Remember to breathe. One of the worst things you can do when you contract your PC muscle (or do any other form of weight training, for that matter) is to hold your breath. This deprives your muscle of oxygen at the point it needs it most, which means the muscle will not be able to work as hard as it has the potential to.

As you do your workout, skipping two days between sessions, you'll notice your PC muscle getting stronger every time you do it.

I recommend keeping track of your times. You'll be impressed with the improvement you make.

By the way, do make sure to allow your PC muscle ample time to rest and recuperate. If you work the muscle out too often, you risk overtraining it, which actually makes it weaker because it hasn't had time to rebuild itself.

This is the exact same thing that happens if you do bench presses every day. If your chest muscles don't get a chance to repair themselves, you'll get weaker not stronger. That's why serious weightlifters give each muscle group time to recuperate after their workouts.

With a strong PC muscle, you'll be able to ejaculate with much greater force, and your refractory periods will go way down. You'll have little trouble achieving powerful erections, virtually on command.

Conclusion: Sex So Good... She'll Beg You For More!

Having bedded literally dozens of women, I have cracked the code on what makes good sex, and I've explained it thoroughly I hope.

As a conclusion, I will sum up my Roadmap for Good Sex for you, nice and simply. Get it right, and you and your woman will have more sex and better sex... and she will adore you as the best lover she's ever had.

The Number One Rule: Don't Try
Be outcome independent and don't even think about whether your woman comes or not. Every woman is capable of having an orgasm. But not every time she has sex. And not with every guy.

But that doesn't matter... women don't need to orgasm to enjoy sex.

When you put your penis into your woman's vagina, all you're doing is caressing the inside of her vagina with it. She gets emotional comfort from that.

At the same time, it feels good to you. Stay focused on the present moment and the awesome sensations you're feeling through your penis.

Think of sex merely as something you do for your own enjoyment and pleasure. Whenever your mind drifts during sex, refocus it on the awesome feelings you're getting.

So stop caring about your "performance."

The Biggest Secret to Master the Art of Sex

You don't make love to your woman with your penis alone. You're also making love to her mind.

When you have sex with her brain at the same time, she feels extremely comfortable and lets herself by vulnerable to you. Women have described it to me as being a "hypnotic, levitating feeling."

So let yourself go. Yeah, you can ingrain the right sexual techniques (and this book is chalk full of them) into your mind, but then forget them.

Instead let your desire run wild and allow your natural instincts to move you.

Stop thinking. Enjoy how intense and powerful your moments are with your woman.

Sex isn't something you need a PhD for. In fact it's the total opposite... your primal nature. Let that nature run wild, and enjoy the endless sex!

Other Guides By John Alexander

How to Become an Alpha Male - Discover how to overcome the biggest mistakes men make when it comes to dating. Check it out at http://AlphaMaleSystem.com

Printed in the United States
209385BV00001B/262/A